DISPLAY

IN THE

CLASSROOM

Principles, Practice and Learning Theory

Hilary Cooper, Penny Hegarty,
Phil Hegarty and Neil Simco

David Fulton Publishers

London

David Fulton Publishers Ltd
2 Barbon Close, London WCIN 3JX

First published in Great Britain by David Fulton Publishers in 1996

British Library Cataloguing in Publication Data

A catalogue record for this book is available from the British Library

ISBN 1-85346-404-X

Typeset by The Harrington Consultancy Ltd
Printed in Great Britain by the Cromwell Press Ltd, Melksham

Contents

Note
A number of illustrations are in colour. They appear together on pp.29–32, and
references to these pages are given, as appropriate, in the text.

Acknowledgements

The four chapters in this book are the result of teachers, student teachers, tutors and children working together to explore the relationship between the processes of learning and display in the classroom. Without their hard work and enthusiasm it could not have been written; their help, support, ready co-operation and permission to use photographs is greatly appreciated. In particular, thanks are due to the staff and children of Fishermoss Primary School, Aberdeen, Gascoigne Infant and Junior Schools, Barking, Settle CP School, Yorkshire, and Levens Primary School, Kendal, Cumbria; and to the students and former students of the Department of Teaching and Education Studies at Lancaster University.

Finally the authors are grateful to Thora Cartwright, who typed their manuscripts with unfailing patience and good humour and with meticulous care, and to Marion Blake for her editing help.

Introduction

This book grew out of our common interest in exploring and articulating the connections between display, learning theory and reflective practice. We define display broadly as the process of creating and responding to the physical environment of the classroom and the school. The need for a book such as this has become more urgent in these times of budget restraints and the need to justify the time and other resources that are allocated to pedagogy and practice. We endorse display as a central and integral part of the teaching and learning process.

Concern with display has a long history, and although our understanding of the complex ways in which children interact with and learn from the classroom environment has come a long way in the last century, when I look at my grandmother's copy of A.H. Garlick's *New Manual of Method*, published in 1896, I find much that resonates with my own experience and intentions.

The importance of a pleasant physical environment was stressed even then. Here is A.H. Garlick, beginning on page four as he means to go on:

Schoolroom Decoration
Walls. These should be clean, and painted a light French grey or pale buff. The lower part should be of wood panelling, or, better still, of dark glazed bricks, so as to form a dado.
Windows. There should be an abundance of window space. Nothing tends to brighten a room like this.

Opportunities to learn from pictures, maps and diagrams around the room were recognised:

Pictures. Pictures of foreign scenes are interesting and instructive, especially those dealing with primitive forms of life, like the African, the Indian, and the Esquimaux. A few good pictures, copies of our best masters' works, might be added. Historic pictures are very interesting to children, and are all the brighter for being coloured. Pictures of trades, brightly coloured, are also very instructive, and very interesting, whilst a few well-chosen Scripture prints should always find a place.
Maps. Picture maps are bright and instructive, preparing the way for the ordinary maps. Of those hanging on the walls, the ordinary ones should be bright-coloured, and should be removed as soon as they become dilapidated or dirty. In such a condition they are little good mentally, and positively bad morally. A few blank maps should be included among the wall decorations.
Diagrams. These will include geographical diagrams for the teaching of definitions; astronomical diagrams for lessons on the sun, moon, and stars; botanical diagrams for botany lessons; mechanical diagrams for lessons on

mechanics; zoological, for lessons on animals, and so on. The choice of these diagrams will be regulated by the school curriculum.

And there was an opportunity to value pupils' achievements:

Honour Board. This should form a most appreciated portion of the wall decorations of a school.

The emphasis since then has increasingly been on learning through interaction with the environment, and as current literature demonstrates, classroom environments have reflected this understanding. Margaret Jackson (1993:9) describes display as 'offering opportunities to stimulate thinking and research and to create, to experiment and design'. Greenstreet (1985:2) identified six purposes of display :

● to make the environment more attractive
● to communicate ideas and information clearly
● to stimulate interest and questioning
● to show appreciation of children's work
● to respond to the interests of the children
● to reflect the general ethos of the school

Makoff and Duncan (1986) stress the importance of displays in inviting children to 'stop, look, touch, talk, question and think', and the potential to involve children in planning and decision-making at all stages. Corbin (1970) saw exhibitions of artefacts in school as playing an important part in education, giving children exciting visual and other experiences, developing their aesthetic sensibilities and providing 'useful points of interest which can inform the basis for thought, speech and expression through various media'. The display of children's work has long been appreciated by teachers as a means of communicating that our schools are places of warmth and care, interest and beauty, excitement and fascination, learning and growth – to child, teacher, parent and visitor alike (Greenstreet 1985).

Why then another book on display when its importance, at least in primary schools, is widely recognised? There are two main reasons. The first is concerned with changing attitudes to primary education and the constraints these are imposing on teachers' time, children's time and resources. There has always been a lay assumption that display is 'wallpaper' and some politicians and their experts maintain that there has been too much 'pleasantness and paint in primary schools'. The current emphasis on local management of schools, economy, testing in core subjects, league tables, and detailed accounting for curriculum hours not only endorses the wallpaper view, it also reduces the time teachers have available to spend on display, regardless of their professional commitment to its value. Creating a display can be extremely time-consuming; it is understandable that many teachers reluctantly give it a low priority. When the National Curriculum has to be fitted into limited contact time with pupils, the thought of providing constantly changing displays can seem overwhelming.

The second reason is that these pressures and anxieties are already being reflected in the questions student teachers ask about display techniques and organization. They reveal an underlying uncertainty which can only be addressed if display is seen as an integral part of a framework based on learning theory. Questions about technique and organisation include:

- Should all displays have the same layout?
- Labelling: handwritten, typed or a mixture? Should different types of writing be used?
- Colour coordination: what are appropriate guidelines for children?
- Can there be too much on the walls?
- Is double mounting necessary? Is there a cheap alternative?
- How often should displays be changed?
- Should a display be 'done all at once'? How do you avoid acres of empty wall space?
- How do you make it less time consuming? What about resources?
- I appreciate that artefacts are important, but how do you stop them 'vanishing'?

Other questions are concerned with the children's part in creating, mounting and labelling displays:

- Does the initial standard matter?
- How much of children's time should be involved?
- How can teachers intervene without taking over?
- Should displays only be topic-related?
- How can a multicultural display be created when the school is not multicultural and resources are difficult to obtain? Are there resource centres?
- Should displays be interactive? How do you achieve this?
- How much should be the children's work?
- Does every child's work need to be included?

These questions show that, even after spending ten weeks with their teacher tutors, student teachers had no coherent understanding of the ways in which the design of the classroom environment can be rooted in theories about how children learn. However, as students monitored and evaluated their displays, they showed an implicit awareness of principles such as the need for children to interact with displays and to claim ownership of them.

Here is one student teacher's evaluation as she looked at photographs of a sequence of five displays she initiated during the year.

- This display lacks an overriding theme. It doesn't mean much to the children.
- This display is getting better, but there are no examples of children's work. I should have used lower case
- A colourful, interactive display. The children have to link parts of the food web with string.
- The children designed and made this habitat display board themselves in one afternoon. It's three-dimensional and shows what they have learned.
- We used this display to consolidate our work. The labels are removable and we had regular quizzes.

Although there is evidence here of the student increasingly evaluating the contribution of each display to the children' learning, there is no conscious and consistent underlying rationale.

This book, then, aims to show in a coherent way how classroom display can reflect theories and research about how children learn, so that teachers can firstly justify resources, their time and the children's time spent on display, as central to the learning process, and secondly so that the allocated time and resources can be used to best advantage. The answers to the students' questions will be addressed in this context.

Each chapter uses actual classroom displays to illustrate the practical results of applying the principles and theoretical frameworks.

In Chapter 1, I draw on my own experience as a primary school teacher and co-ordinator of art in a variety of London schools, particularly Greenvale Primary School, Croydon. More recent examples come from the work of student teachers and classroom teachers in London and in Cumbria.

Neil Simco is fortunate in that his wife, Samantha Simco, is a teacher of a Year 3, 4 and 5 class in Levens C.E. School, in Cumbria. They have used a term's work on Hadrian's Wall not only to observe, record and photograph the development of the project, but to articulate and explore Samantha's reflection-in-action and reflection-on-action within a framework of the negotiated classroom.

Phil Hegarty in Chapter 3 has used the work and reflection of Helen O'Neill during her student teacher practice with Mrs J. Murdoch at Grange C.E. Primary School to illustrate the possibilities of task analysis in an ongoing spiral of thoughtful practice that has much in common with action research.

Penny Hegarty conducted a series of interviews with children in some of the classrooms she visited as a tutor. She analysis the transcripts of three interviews within the framework of theories of perception.

It will be clear that our ways of thinking and working have been much influenced by two scholars, one American and one British. Donald Schön has developed the theories of reflecting-in-action and reflecting-on-action that are influential in professional development and teacher education. John Elliott has both critiqued and affirmed Schön's original work and has woven it into his ongoing extension and exploration of action research in teacher education.

CHAPTER 1

It's Not Just Wallpaper: a constructivist framework for classroom display

Hilary Cooper

The need to create a constructivist framework for display corresponds to the need to produce a framework of professional competences. Teachers once argued that, although they have a 'gut feeling' about what makes a good teacher, and about what a 'lively classroom' looks like, these qualities are too subjective for precise definition or consensus. An increasing body of research and the need for professional accountability have shown that this is not the case. This chapter describes and analyses five common approaches to display and the need for a constructivist framework for creating and evaluating the classroom environment. Then we shall consider the key elements of constructivist learning theory and how these relate to classroom display. Examples of different categories of display will be evaluated using this framework. Finally the design of a whole-school policy reflecting these principles will be considered.

FIVE APPROACHES TO DISPLAY

Some approaches to display reflect aspects of learning theory in a piecemeal way. Others may inhibit learning. All have been enthusiastically admired by some colleagues and castigated by others, for inconsistent reasons. These approaches may be grouped under the following headings: intuitive, illustrative, training the hand and eye, the Arts and Crafts Movement style, and the economy model. We have probably all experienced most of these categories at some time.

The intuitive approach

Until recently it was widely believed that certain individuals were born to teach, not trained and educated for teaching. Indeed I began my career in primary education after applying to the London County Council for a post as a secondary school history teacher. They asked if I would be prepared to teach infants instead as there was a desperate shortage. And so I arrived at 8.45 a.m. on the first day of term, at a school where the headteacher was also new. She took me to a class of 38 six-year-olds, where she thought 'I could do least damage', for as she told me 'We don't like people like you in infant schools'. The other staff members were set in their ways and their pupils existed on a diet of sum cards and 'Janet and John' readers.

The new head felt that the learning of the children in this inner-city school would be improved if each day began with 'activities'. This decision was not welcomed by the staff who felt that 'Children are only awake and able to work first thing in the morning'. They fulfilled this prophecy by beginning the day with raucous races around the hall with doll prams, carts and cars. For those insufficiently extrovert for such 'activities', the desultory cutting up of pictures or making of jigsaws was provided.

Partly to ingratiate, but also because I had been dipping into the work of Piaget (1954), Isaacs (1930) and Kellog (1969) with great interest, I planned my 'activities' sessions differently. The children had enjoyed the story of the Pied Piper. The next morning when they arrived they found frieze paper across the back of the room, trays of paint in shades of blue and grey and cut potatoes on the table, ready to paint the sky and the cobbled streets of Hamelin. On another table was the glue and a selection of papers for a group of children to make the houses of Hamelin. As the week progressed the collage grew: rats of every shade and variety of whisker and tail, then children too – everyone could join in with pictures of themselves and their friends processing along the potato print cobbles. Success led to success and the room became alive with activity, enthusiasm and independence. As a student teacher recently wrote of her own work

> The display certainly had an affect on me and I feel that this was not too dissimilar from the way it affected the children. For example I felt a sense of ownership although the work was the childrens.

I wrote the lines of the story beneath the collage and the children spontaneously began to use these words to write about their own drawings. They decided to write a big book. Lots of little books followed, and drama, and counting.

Fired by this obvious success – the children were interested and well-behaved and were clearly learning all sorts of language and number skills – the next 'activities' sessions focused on a greengrocer's shop and creating papier mâché fruit and vegetables and tissue paper flowers. The children made posters and price labels and 'props' were begged from the greengrocer's over the road. This led to number work, weighing, counting and money sums. By Christmas the headteacher was showing it all off to her colleagues. My aims had been to prove that she *did* like people like me in her school, to survive, and to enjoy myself – in that order. No sound basis in constructivist theory here – or was there?

Of course this is not innovative practice now but it took place in 1963, interestingly the year in which Sybil Marshall wrote *An Experiment in Education* which foreshadowed changes in the philosophy aims and methods of primary education (later to be endorsed by the Plowden Report, DES, 1967). Yet Sybil Marshall evolved her approach gradually and naturally. She defined it as a belief :

- that to have the greatest beneficial effect, any experience the child gains must bear some relation to what he understands already, and be such that further new experiences can be added to it. This means it may have to be individual.
- that children are geared towards growing up: they seek maturing experience. Their curiosity, ingenuity, creative ability and boundless energy are the tools they employ to obtain such experience. They are by nature motivated to learn when the learning situation is one of exploration and discovery; (it is most important to remember in this context that it is equally 'natural' for them to want to practise skills of all kinds until they have mastered them).
- that education occurs in situations based on experience and active individual participation.

There is no index to Sybil Marshall's book, no references to learning theory. Indeed the English translation of Vygotsky's *Thought and Language* was only published in 1962 and Bruner's *The Process of Education* in 1963. To some extent Sybil Marshall's work precedes rather than draws on learning theory, yet she was not alone in her understanding that children learn through experience, based on curiosity about what they already know. The classroom environments she and her children created reflected these principles. That is why I have used the Pied Piper display as an example of the 'intuitive approach'.

The illustrative approach

The displays in this category are the equivalent of illustrating a book on the Civil War with a picture of Cromwell's hat: there is no suggestion as to how that hat might prompt significant questions or inferences. I was guilty frequently as a part-time teacher, when I was asked to 'take out groups to do the art', (i.e. the messy part) of the class 'topic'. The resulting product was related to the theme only by content because I had no idea how the topic was being taught. The display was discrete. It did not arise from learning, and did not reflect or extend it; it did not stem from the children's ideas or involve them in choices. Nevertheless they greatly enjoyed doing it and it was highly valued, presumably because it was usually interesting. A life-size effigy of a Cavalier with curled black paper hair was exhibited at the Camden Arts Centre. A jewel-encrusted collage of the Taj Mahal, made by a class of ten-year-olds, was displayed in an up-market antiques shop selling Indian furniture, in return for a substantial contribution to school funds. A sound basis in learning theory would have enabled this work to be created and extended in so many other rich and educationally valid ways.

It is interesting, too, how changing perspectives influence content, and the need to justify its selection, using pedagogically valid criteria. I blush to think of much admired collages of 'people around the world': the 'Eskimo' made because of the opportunity it allowed for five-year olds to stick on all the cotton wool, the 'Red Indian' because of all the feathers and the 'African' who was festooned with wonderful beads made by winding card around paintbrush handles. The 1960s were not as distant from A. H. Garlick's 1896 manual as we imagined at the time.

Training the hand and eye

The heavy hand of the teacher imposed on children's ownership and creativity is still common in the classroom environment. It is seen in the templates which are 'cut around carefully' and filled in 'without going over the edges', in the sterile, teacher-drawn outlines, and the displays made from the chopped-out 'good bits' of children's pictures. This kind of work devalues and often destroys children's own rich, creative and unique responses to their world. It seems to derive from the manuals of 'Hand and Eye Training' used by my grandmother (Bevis, 1895) which were based on the principle that 'the child be actively employed in training his hands to neatness, accuracy and correct obedience to the dictates of the eye ... A small portion of correct and neat methods and accurate and careful work should be the ambition of the teacher'. It shows no respect for children's own representational systems which were categorized by Kellog (1969) and inspired the subsequent the research of Arnheim (1974) and Goodrow (1977, 1978) among others.

I was confronted with this approach to display (in my view a truly destructive one) when I was appointed to a post of responsibility for 'art and display throughout the school'. By that time I had become interested in such questions as what is art, why does it matter, why do children want to create images of the world, are there developmental patterns in the ways in which they do so, and how can their images be evaluated? Clearly these are huge questions far beyond the remit of this book, but they did leave me very much aware that classroom environments should reflect children's individual images of and responses to the world they observe, and their attempts to make sense of it.

Descartes' view was that art communicates each individual's perceptions of their environment and feelings, by using their own marks to create a relationship with the environment based on internal and external ordering of feelings. Art therefore develops both an individual's uniqueness and each individual's responsibility for their own perceptions and images of the world. It is concerned with fulfilment and can create a shared experience and challenge for both teachers and children. It involves problem-solving and emotional and intellectual life. Einstein said that we alter the outside world by our thinking about it. As a Schools Council booklet (1978) has said, drawing is an outward-looking search for an inward-looking retrieval system. Recent research suggests that there is not a clear developmental pattern based on children's concern to show perspective but that children's drawings are developed from an 'optic array'. They are concerned with spatial relationships other than perspectives (Willatts, 1981). Children may be developing sophisticated structuring syntax as young as two- to four-years old (Matthews 1983), and such syntax is culture dependent. It is used to describe narratives, time sequences, objects and fantasy.

Of course display is involved with the whole curriculum, not just art. But because display is largely dependent on visual images, it is important to consider the power of art in reflecting the way each individual responds to experiences and tries to understand and record them. Display also reflects theories about how we assimilate, internalize, construct and reconstruct our understanding of the world through constant interaction.

On this basis, in my new role as coordinator for art and display, I discussed with colleagues plans for the 'new hall pictures' and was amazed at the response, a spirited justification for yet more teacher drawn outlines 'filled in' by the children. 'We have standards here' I was told. Children's work might be alright in the classroom, but not in the hall. I never succeeded in convincing them that templates devalue children's dynamic, vivid, personal responses, destroy their uniqueness and their ability to question. This was some years ago and yet only recently I could not convince a student teacher that a chain of 38 coloured-in outlines of Nellie the Elephant was not destructive. Their purpose was, she said, 'to teach number, not art'.

The Arts and Craft Movement style

This approach had its roots in particular teacher training institutions throughout the 1970s and 1980s. It has a carefully thought out rationale based on the philosophy of William Morris and the Arts and Crafts Movement.

The educational ideals are of the highest. Draw children's attention to beauty in natural objects (a feather, a shell, a seed head), and in simple functional artefacts made from natural materials (stone, wool, clay, wood). 'Art', Rilke said 'rekindles the commonplace'. It develops sensitivity, both intellectually and aesthetically, to structure and form, to patterns, rhythms and colour, by meticulous observation, recorded in carefully observed drawings. These observations can be developed in other media: pen and ink with water colour wash; lino prints on paper and cloth; weaving using wool carded by the children, spun on wheels or hand spindles and dyed with natural dyes; pottery. with oxide glazes. Teach children, through intimate handling, to appreciate the inherent qualities of materials and to develop skills in selecting and using appropriate tools. Watch craftspersons at work making fences and furniture, shearing sheep, creating hand-made books. This work reflected an integrated holistic approach to the curriculum and classroom organisation based on an integrated day, in which groups of children could use the specialized equipment needed for batik, screen printing, pottery and many other crafts.

Although this philosophy was initially based on respect for children as individuals, and for the processes of learning through responding to and making sense of the environment in active ways, the approach became learned by many student teachers as a recipe, only partially understood and so not capable of growth or interpretation. Whole swathes of schools, often in harsh urban environments, were transformed by what became a style of classroom display of a very high standard, but such displays all bore the hallmarks of a recipe. The recipe consisted of triple mounting on black, grey or beige paper using dressmakers pins, a concern for sight-lines and exquisite calligraphy, a 'sympathetic drape' in hand printed fabric, a plant, a beautiful artefact or natural object, and possibly a hand-made book.

Classroom environments were based on a clearly recognizable style which was both inspiring and seductive but because it was based on a style it became ossified and predictable. It ceased to reflect different modes of learning, different ways and levels of understanding, different curriculum areas, and children's choices and decisions. It was a style imposed by adults, although the work was the children's. Children ceased to respond, because the style was always the same, and parents, because they did not see it as significant in children's learning, did not value it either.

The economy model

This is in danger of becoming wide-spread in the current economic climate; it is based on the notion that money spent on mounting paper is a waste of money or a waste of trees. I have known students mount work on newspaper for this reason. Since no one would wish to encourage waste or the damaging of the hillsides, it is essential to firstly take reasonable measures such as trimming, storing and re-using pinned mounts and to recognize that not everyone's work needs to be on display; there are other ways of valuing work. But more importantly it is essential to justify resources used in creating the learning environment as central to and essential to the processes of learning.

A CONSTRUCTIVIST FRAMEWORK

If display and the physical classroom environment is to be justified as an essential and integral part of children's learning it must reflect key theory about how children learn. Although their theories continue to be modified, developed and refined, the key learning theorists are still Jean Piaget, Jerome Bruner and Lev Vygotsky. It is important to recognize the differences between them, but also what they have in common.

What is a constructivist framework?

Piaget is not always regarded as a constructivist because he outlined a universal pattern of qualitative stages of development moving from thinking dominated by intuitive trial and error and a child's own experiences and feelings, to a stage when a child is able to form deductions based on concrete experiences, then finally to thinking in purely abstract terms. However, since the constructivist position is that children construct their own views of reality from their unique experiences, his ideas and theirs are not incompatible. Piaget shows throughout his work how children learn by observing their physical environment and interacting with it, often by manipulating objects. In doing so they form hypotheses, test them and draw conclusions. They assimilate these conclusions into their own mental maps or *schemata* of the world and reapply them to new situations. When they come across a situation which conflicts with their existing framework they have to adjust it to accommodate the new information or experience. In this way they constantly form, consolidate and reform their understanding in the light of their experiences.

In broad terms Piaget's analysis of the learning process is still valid, although it has been modified. Margaret Donaldson (1978) for example showed the extent to which young children's ability to solve problems depends on discussing the meanings of words, on understanding the problem and on whether the problem stems from their own concerns, or is a physical situation they can relate to.

Bruner (1966) also stressed the importance of learning through interacting with the environment. He suggested three ways of representing and responding to it which he saw to some extent as developmental, but as overlapping rather than rigidly sequential. He suggested that at first children learn largely kinetically, that is through physical exploration, investigating how things are made, how they work, how they are used. Later they learn through making and responding to visual images – pictures, maps, diagrams. The third way of exploring and making sense of the world is through symbolic systems; through number systems – and particularly through language. Bruner (1963) believed that the materials children are given must be carefully selected to actively stimulate children's interest and take into account their previous experience. Material should be selected so that general principles can be inferred from specific examples, connections can be made and detail placed in a structured pattern which is not forgotten. A young child must be given minimal information, but the emphasis must be on showing the child how to go beyond it. Experiences, materials and questions must therefore be selected carefully, and children encouraged to handle and experiment with objects.

Vygotsky (1962) also traced a pattern of cognitive development but his central concern was concept development. He showed that this is a deductive process; concepts are learned not through ready-made definitions but by abstracting common characteristics by trial and error, based initially on experience of the physical world. At the first stage objects are grouped by chance. At the second stage they are linked by one characteristic which can change as new information is added. Gradually 'pseudo concepts' develop which are deduced from context and are stable, although the child may be thinking of the concept in a different way from an adult. At the final stage a child is able to formulate a rule which establishes a relationship between concepts. Vygotsky found that concepts explicitly selected and taught are understood better than those used incidentally. This pattern of development has been endorsed and explained further by Ausubel (1963, 1968), Gagne (1977), Klausmeier (1978, 1979) and others.

Klausmeier (1979) found that children learn concepts both through verbal labelling related to tactile examples and to imagery; the word and the images are stored, and shared characteristics abstracted; new information can then be added and generalizations made. There is also evidence that verbal cues and discussion help children to sort and to recognize shared characteristics; that categories are learned more rapidly when people are initially exposed only to typical examples; and that other information tends to be stored around concepts.

There are two ways in which theories of concept development relate to classroom display and learning environments. First there are often opportunities for making collections related to a theme. This may be a collection of objects, of pictures or of words written on cards. If these can be physically manipulated, and sorted and resorted through discussion, children can develop the key vocabulary related to a discipline or to a theme within it, at both concrete and over-arching levels. The sorting for young children may be into hoops or boxes; older children can use large Venn or Carol diagrams to sort objects, words or pictures related to a curriculum area. Either specific examples can be collected which reflect given labels, (old, new, light, heavy) or labels can be devised which reflect shared attributes (castles with a keep, with a mound, in Britain, in fairy stories). Sets can be constantly subdivided and refined: materials, metals, different metals. Collections of words on cards can be made and sorted in response to a shared experience or in preparation for descriptive writing. Young children can make collections of pictures of objects that begin with the same sound, for a quiz and word bank. Concept development can also be encouraged in the way wall displays are organized.

They can show the relationships between selected key concepts used and introduced in class lessons. Or children can use thread and pins to build up and rearrange concept maps as a topic progresses.

Piaget acknowledged the need for discussion and interaction in learning and both Vygotsky and Bruner saw the growth of understanding as an eventually collective and collaborative process. Vygotsky (1978) saw learning as occurring through assisted performance which enables children to perform at higher developmental levels than they can independently, by interaction with others who have a greater degree of competence. He defined this process as consisting of four stages: assistance by others who are more capable (parents, teachers, experts, peers); self assistance which involves increased understanding; internalization of the new ability; and finally further self assistance. Vygotsky called this cyclical process of learning (self help through assistance from others) the 'zone of proximal development'. Assistance from others can be in many forms: body language, demonstration, suggesting materials, giving information, revisiting, asking questions, giving clues, indicating choices or help in structuring tasks. It may be frequent, or increasingly infrequent. Bruner (1983:60) described this process as 'scaffolding', 'one sets the game, provides a scaffold to assume that the child's ineptitudes can be rescued and then removes the scaffold, part by part as the reciprocal structure can stand on its own'.

A great deal of subsequent research has investigated how cognitive growth may come about through children interacting with their peers, either as a result of conflicting viewpoints or different cognitive levels (Doise *et al.*, 1975; Perret Clermont, 1980). The effects of social interaction on children's thinking at different ages and in different situations is still being assessed. There is accumulating evidence that for five- to nine-year olds shared responsibility for planning with a peer or an adult results in cognitive gains (Gauvain and Rogoff, 1989); that benefits are more likely to accrue to those whose partner is more competent (Tudge, 1992); and also that while children do learn from each other they learn more from collaboration which also involves an adult's participation in planning and guidance (Radziszewska and Rogoff, 1991).

IMPLICATIONS OF CONSTRUCTIVIST THEORY FOR CLASSROOM DISPLAY

Displays should encourage children, individually or collaboratively to :

Observe their environment

- outside school (the natural and the man-made environment, and people)
- inside the school grounds, (pet area, school garden, pond, adventure area)
- in the common school space (foyer, corridor, special curriculum and resource areas)

- in the classroom (objects, pictures and photographs selected to stimulate curiosity and related to the intended learning)

Question

- what
- why
- how
- where
- when?

Investigate

- in different artistic media
- in quizzes and games
- in research
- through data collection in surveys, questionnaires.
- through physical manipulation of objects (how was it made, used, how does it work?)
- through the senses (how does it feel, smell, taste, sound?)
- through social interaction (making and using role play areas, creating displays, making collaborative images and models)

Observation, questioning and investigation will enable children to challenge, extend and change their existing understandings. To achieve this, the classroom environment must be *planned* as an integral part of the content and process of the learning of all the children. Display is a dynamic process that extends and evolves over time.

Table 1.1 shows how a dynamic classroom environment can be planned as an intrinsic part of a scheme of work. Tables 1.2 and 1.3 show how the implications arising from constructivist theories can be related to National Curriculum requirements. (These are suggestions, not a comprehensive list.) The column headed 'Display Examples' is left blank so that display

Table 1.1 Display: an integral part of medium-term planning					
TASK/ ACTIVITIES (showing progression)	Learning intentions (code and refer those elements of POS identified in your scheme). Concepts, knowledge, skills, processes, attitudes	Relevant Attainment Targets, Level Descriptions and other assessment foci	Formative and diagnostic Assessment Opportunities and Intentions - eg observation, product, discussion, questioning	Classroom Environment Displays T. provided? Children's work? Purposes? Whose display?	Resources Checklist

Table 1.2 Display in relation to National Curriculum Key Stage 1

Main implications of constructivist theory of learning for display at Key Stage 1:

- Immediacy; respond to children's present interests, activities, stimuli.
- Enactive; opportunities to explore through manipulation.
- Sensory; opportunities to feel, smell (taste) hear.
- Concept development; attention to grouping and naming pictures/artefacts with shared attributes and labelling with overarching concept.
- Attention to language used in labelling, responding, discussing, to questions asked and meanings of words.
- Emphasis on children's individual responses to a display.

LEARNING THEORY	DISPLAY IMPLICATIONS	DISPLAY EXAMPLES	REFERENCES TO NATIONAL CURRICULUM

1. Piaget
Child's thinking characterised by egocentricity; not concerned to interest or convince others, preoccupation with own feelings and by the senses.
 	
Art
Characterised by own schema; size and perspective dominated by the affective.
 	
Play
Pleasurable, simultaneous characterised by symbolic objects.
	Frequently changed. Immediate to experience or interest.
	- Objects children can touch individually,
	  – hear (pitch, timbre)
	  feel (texture, weight)
	explore through lenses, coloured film, telescopes etc.
	- Respect for children's own images.
	Sensory art (finger painting, modelling)
	- Role play areas (post office, cafe, dentist, etc Teacher's stimuli but not intervention.
			History
			Children should be taught about people, events in the past, in Britain and from other cultures.
			
			Science
			Sound, light, lenses.
			
			Music/Science
			Group according to pitch, timbre, smooth, tinkling, ringing etc.
			
			Art
			Record observations, experiences, feelings.
			
			English
			Read information related to experience and beyond, which has accessible themes and ideas; language with repetitive patterns and rhyme, related to visually stimulating illustrations. Develop phonic and graphic knowledge. Opportunities for drama activities.
			
			Art
			Recognising images.

Table 1.2 cont.

LEARNING THEORY	DISPLAY IMPLICATIONS	DISPLAY EXAMPLES	REFERENCE TO NATIONAL CURRICULUM
Donaldson *(et al)* Children can reason and change perspective in everyday situations, if they are interested and understand the language. They need to discuss the meanings of words and recognise the abstraction of language.	Familiar images which children can explain, question. Sequence (eg of pictures from a story;) Paintings Drawings Photographs		*Geography* What is it? Where is it? What is it like? How did it get like this? (about locality another town or country). Describe features, farms, parks, rivers, towns, factories. *History* Children can reason about everyday situations (clothes, diet, buildings etc) and should be helped to go beyond this to compare with similar situations in other times. *I.T.* Communicate information in text, tables, pictures. *Science* How, why, what will happen if ...? (domestic objects/circuits).
2. Bruner *Enactive Representation* Children learn through physical experience and manipulation. Teachers should select experiences, materials, question carefully and show children how to go beyond these. The key questions and ideas of any curriculum area can be translated into a form which children can grapple with from the very beginning.	Artefacts which work: toys, tools, instruments: to explore, investigate, use; made from materials basic to civilisations; woods, metals, clay, sand, water, wool, leather and man made materials: plastics, fabrics. Children's models, construction toys, junk models.		*Technology* Shape, assemble, rearrange materials and components, models and pictures to develop and communicate designs. Suggest improvements, explain what they are making. *Art* Use variety of media, recognise artefacts, experiment with tools and techniques.
3. Vygotsky *Concept Development* Objects with shared characteristics linked by chance. Shared characteristic changes as new information is introduced. Concepts learned through labelling, images, direct experience. Intermediate categories learned first. Prototypes are remembered. Concept development promoted by selecting concepts and using them, and by discussing similarities and differences.	Shapes, colours, images, artefacts and materials to 'sort', describe reasons for sets. Use of prepositions on labels (e.g. under, over, above, below, through) related to physical experiences (e.g. bricks, junk models) or to pictures. Labels for groups of objects: pictures, photographs giving names to group in relation to relevant overarching concepts eg different types of: chairs, toys, shells, leaves or summer/winter, hot/cold, heavy/light.		*History* Sequence events and objects, sort into eg old/new; before/after. Make deductions and inferences about artefacts; how they were made/used. *Maths* Represent work with objects and pictures; recognise and make use of a simple pattern based on experience, represent work as symbols and diagrams (ask what would happen if?).

Table 1.2 cont.

LEARNING THEORY	DISPLAY IMPLICATIONS	DISPLAY EXAMPLES	REFERENCE TO NATIONAL CURRICULUM
			Use and interpret mathematical symbols and diagrams. Explore/name properties of 2-D/3-D shapes. Sort and classify: shape, size, colour, height and other maths concepts according to one or more criteria. Make tables, graphs, diagrams and interpret, count sets of objects. *Science* Scientific vocabulary e.g. parts of body, of plants. Similarities and differences between selves and other pupils, group according to babies/children/adults, group living things according to observed differences. *Art* Sets of colour, pattern, texture. Select and sort images and artefacts, according to old/new, different cultures, similarities and differences in craft and design. *Geography* Traffic surveys.

Table 1.3 Display in relation to National Curriculum Key Stage 2

LEARNING THEORY	DISPLAY IMPLICATIONS	DISPLAY EXAMPLES	REFERENCE TO NATIONAL CURRICULUM
1. Piaget Child is able to take in visible and tangible information (and knowledge from other sources), store it, and retrieve it selectively to apply to new problems. Reasoned premises are followed by deductions and inferences. Children are increasingly aware of what can be known and what can be guessed (of estimating/calculating probability). Conjunctions used to justify assertions: because, since, therefore. Children are concerned to explain an argument and to convince others. When new information or experience does not fit into existing thinking patterns these are adjusted in response to the challenge. Children have a rigid and unquestioning acceptance of rules.	Displays can be built up over longer periods. They are based on children's hypotheses and enquiries. These arise from children's experiences of their visible and tangible environment. Children are able to collect and store information to support an enquiry or investigation. They can discuss contradictory or unexpected findings and results, attempt to explain them to others, and change their understanding in doing so. Children are eager to explain and justify their findings, arguments and points of view to others, in a wall display, exhibition, presentation.		*Geography* Observe, ask questions, collect evidence, draw conclusions about places: why they are there, how people live there, influence of people on natural and man-made environment and vice versa. *Science* Focused explanations, investigation. *Maths* Probability, identify and obtain information to solve problems, organise and discuss work and explain thinking. *History* Find out about and compare past and present and different periods of the past, recall, select and organise information. Identify and give reasons why past is represented in different ways. Make links between main events and changes within and across periods. *English* Opportunities to explore, explain and develop ideas, read aloud, share, report; to communicate to different audiences; challenging subject matter that broadens and extends thinking. Pose problematic questions about a topic they are investigating, distinguish between fact and opinion. Present information in different forms.

Table 1.3 Cont.

LEARNING THEORY	DISPLAY IMPLICATIONS	DISPLAY EXAMPLES	REFERENCE TO NATIONAL CURRICULUM
Role Play The goals of play may be extrinsic to either the adult or the child, or to both. Instruction, exploration, fantasy and problem solving are not necessarily separate. Understanding of the behaviour (attitudes, values, feelings) of others, at present and in other times and places, is an affective as well as a cognitive process. (Piaget 1956, Kohlberg 1976, Jones 1968). Bruner encouraged children to understand the attitudes and values of other societies by exploring, for example how parallel conflict situations are dealt with or basic needs are met in different societies.	Initiate support and extend learning through role play areas based on a topic or programme of study.		*English* Opportunities to participate in drama activities; explore, develop, explain ideas, share insights and opinions, enact stories and poems, present to audiences
Creativity Teachers can develop divergent thinking by setting up an environment in which children are confident in their abilities to think creatively, (e.g. by making a range of suggestions). Guilford (1959); what is this used for? Torrance (1965) what caused this? What happened next? What is happening in this picture? Can you interpret this pattern.	Use of pictures or artefacts, linked to open-ended questions to curriculum areas, possible as a stimulus for introducing a topic.		

Table 1.3 Cont.

LEARNING THEORY	DISPLAY IMPLICATIONS	DISPLAY EXAMPLES	REFERENCE TO NATIONAL CURRICULUM
2. Bruner Dominant mode of representing ideas at heart of a discipline is iconic (although enactive and iconic modes are not rigidly successive). Essence of experience is represented as a picture in the mind's eye. Minimum information should be given and children shown how to go beyond it. Therefore language is important in the symbolic mode of representation, responding to images and promoting cognitive growth. Questions asked should be the key questions of a discipline. (They should not be too simple or too hard). Children need to learn how to formulate and answer such questions. Symbolic representation is the third, but not necessarily sequential mode of representation.	Select drawings, paintings, photographs, maps, diagrams which represent key ideas of a discipline, at an appropriate level. Key questions are linked to these images, and opportunities created for children to answer them in appropriate ways. Children explore and represent their understanding of central ideas of a discipline, through making models, drawing, painting, photographs, diagrams, maps, images in other media; printing, needlework. Children use their understanding of key questions to ask similar questions about the models and images they have made, (e.g. in labelling, questionnaire or quiz) or they can extrapolate from information they find about teacher selected images to write explanations of their own models or images		*Technology* Labelled sketches show details of designs, recognize user preference. Draw on understanding of familiar products. Discuss children's drawings and models, produce step by step plans. *Geography* Where/what is it? What is it like? How did it get like this? Why is it changing? *I.T.* Use IT to organise, refine, present information. *Art* Express ideas and feelings, design and make. *History* Ask questions and make deductions about the past from visual sources, artefacts, buildings, sites, select and record information. *Music* Record compositions using symbols, for other groups to play. *Mathematics* Use symbols, words, diagrams, make 3D models, use related language. *English* Consider an argument critically, opportunities to write for varied purposes, writing is essential to thinking and learning, write for different audiences, recognise characteristics of different kinds of writing.

Table 1.3 Cont.

LEARNING THEORY	DISPLAY IMPLICATIONS	DISPLAY EXAMPLES	REFERENCE TO NATIONAL CURRICULUM
3. Vygotsky *Concept Development* Children increasingly able to discriminate similarities and differences at a concrete level (i.e. pictures or artefacts which can be represented by a visual image). However, these concepts may still be unstable; child may think of the concept in a different way from an adult. Concepts are best learned through visual and tactile examples. Language is essential in concept development to formulate an hypothesis about what is a shared attribute, then to test this by asking questions in sequence (is this an x why/not?), in elaborating on similarities and differences, then to label items belonging to a set, and the shared attribute. Sets may then be combined under an over-arching abstract concept (e.g. sets of trains, of cars, of ships, of bicycles, belong to an over-arching concept, transport). Some specialised concepts are best explicitly taught by being selected, discussed, then used in a variety of contexts.	Opportunities to collect images, artefacts etc on a theme, which have a shared attribute. Arrange, and rearrange (on wall, or table) in sets. Either label the sets formed, or group objects or pictures around a label. Discuss this process with others. Explain reasons for groupings or make up a quiz: what do these all have in common? Or where does this (mystery object) belong? Why? Use selected specialised key vocabulary central to a curriculum area to label. Introduce over-arching abstract concepts, for example in the heading to a display.		*History* Use dates and terms related to the passing of time and concepts related to past times, including abstract concepts e.g. court monarch, parliament, trade, industry, law. *English* Note the meaning of recently encountered words; explain unfamiliar vocabulary. Relevance of word families, roots and origins, spell complex polysyllabic words. *Maths* Collect data, record in bar-charts and diagrams (showing categories of data).

opportunities devised in the planning grid (Table 1.1) can be mapped according to their link with learning theory and the National Curriculum. The categories and examples of display discussed in this book can also be mapped against this framework.

CATEGORIES OF DISPLAY WHICH ARISE FROM A CONSTRUCTIVIST FRAMEWORK

To employ teachers' and children's time effectively and to be integral to children's learning, the display needs to stimulate, arise from and extend the work going on in the classroom, in dynamic and interactive ways. Six categories of display are discussed: stimulus, collections, investigations, collaborative painting (including environments and models), presentations and role play.

Stimulus display

Stimulus displays are created by the teacher, at the beginning of a new term or topic, to make a statement which is both visual and intellectual. It conveys the message that this will be the subject of subsequent work, that the teacher has already given time and thought, and that this will be exciting. Because the display has been carefully selected and presented it is visually stimulating; it also conveys implicit expectations about the quality of work and the attitudes and relationships surrounding it. It need not be time-consuming to create. It may consist of a picture (painting, photograph or poster), an artefact, or a tape recording of a piece of music or a story central to the theme, arranged with a plant, a fabric drape, a question and some means of eliciting responses. The questions will depend on the subject itself and on the further work planned.

Examples of questions:

- What is the rest like? (broken pot)
- What is it used for? How does it work? (artefact)
- Do you like it? Why? (poem, music, painting, book, sound, something to smell or taste)
- What will happen next? (photograph, experiment)
- What is happening outside the picture frame?
- What can we do about this? (emotive, controversial or provocative issues)
- How likely? How many? (mathematics, problems)
- Can you do this? (quiz, puzzle, mathematics investigation, science experiment, e.g. make this fish swim in the bowl drawn on the reverse of card)

Examples of opportunities to respond

- A competition
- A box for suggestions
- A 'wall' to write on
- A tape-recorder to record ideas
- A 'post-card' to reply on

A stimulus display introduces a topic through encouraging questions about it; these reflect and reveal the children's present knowledge and understanding. They are starting points from which teachers can support children in planning their own enquiries in order to extend and perhaps contest their existing understanding. Since teachers have begun by eliciting each child's understanding this can be a useful basis for formative and summative assessments.

Collections

Making collections related to a theme is another quick and effective way of involving children, as well as parents and others, in creating learning environments related to children's own lives and experiences outside school, and also to work places and the broader life of the community. Teachers can then build on these shared individual contributions in numerous ways depending on the topic, the children's ages and the work planned. Some examples of successful collections are:

- *Old things* Some infant classes have begun simply with 'old things'; others have collected old toys, our toys when we were babies, baby clothes, or our photographs, as a basis for further work in ordering, sorting and making inferences. For older children categories related to a history topic can be agreed by children and teacher depending on the planned focuses of the topic. 'Old farm tools' can lead to science investigations about time and energy as part of historical questions about how they were used, why, causes and effects of change, similarities and differences.
- *Treasures* Collected because they are of special significance to children and to teachers, they became the basis of discussions about what we value, and why. This involved discussion of the importance of non-monetary values.
- *Hats* Can be quickly collected and displayed pinned to a wall and involve the lives and experiences of all members of a class. They may also represent occupations of friends and parents and can lead to all sorts of topics about jobs, cultural differences, leisure activities.
- *Clothes* One student teacher, asked to plan work on this theme and desperate to transform a bare Victorian classroom, simply invited everyone to bring in an interesting item of clothing and suspended these

artistically around the walls and from the rafters. A pair of Victorian bloomers was a special attraction. A more focused use of a clothes collection was made in connection with a geography topic on Greece. Children brought to school items they would like to take on holiday to Greece and made a display. In groups they then selected the items they would choose to take on holiday, within their baggage allowance, using a spring balance to weigh each article. This involved considerable discussion and calculation.

- *An archaeological dig* The children initiated this collection by spontaneously deciding to 'excavate' an area of rough ground in the school, after they had watched a television programme on archaeology. They chose to display their collection, ranging from an old shoe and a toy car to a tap and a broken vase, and to make inferential labels, saying what they thought each object was and how it came to be there. These were supported by archaeological drawings and a time-line showing suggested sequence of age.

  This led to further research, in the community and in the library, about the site before the school was built. It demonstrated to the teacher that the children were able to use the processes of historical enquiry and to transfer them to new contexts. It was a quickly created display, initiated by the children, but within the context of the teacher's plans.

- *Patterns in wood and stone* The children made this collection and responded to it in a continuous, dynamic way throughout the term. It was part of a science topic on the properties of materials, but the children became fascinated by the patterns in different kinds of wood and stone. They amassed a collection which involved lugging big slabs of slate, stone, logs and planks to school, and recording the patterns in pencil and charcoal. These drawings were later extended into all kinds of media throughout the term: batik, embroidery, silk screen printing and pottery.

- *Journeys* A collection of walking, pot-holing and climbing gear, maps, photographs and compasses, formed a starting point for cross-curricular work on journeys. This involved geography, science, maths and orienteering. It led on to the children deciding to create a 'caving system' in the classroom by covering tables with blankets. Blindfolded, they tunnelled, one by one in silence through the dark cave system. This half hour of tunnelling had a great impact on the children. They wrote collaboratively about their feelings while pot-holing and also created individual poems and stories. Children frequently returned to the 'pot-hole' for further inspiration.

Investigations

This kind of display really depends on having on-going investigations constantly available and aesthetically presented, perhaps against a background drape, or arranged on fresh coloured paper with some interrogative labels. Investigations can be extended over time as children experiment and discuss and share them, both individually in spare moments and more formally as a class. The following are examples of such investigative displays.

- *Musical instruments*   (Figure 1.1) The focus of enquiry and discussion changed as children first investigated variables of pitch by experimenting with tubes, rubber bands and liquids. They then shared designs for making an instrument which played a sequence of notes of different pitch. Next they made a collection of 'instruments' which were put on display and experimented with. Poems were written and displayed which could be 'accompanied' by the instruments. Finally one group of children decided to make a tape recording explaining to others how the instruments could be made and played. The children initiated each of these stages, within the teacher's framework plans on 'sound'. Again there were constant opportunities for appropriate teacher intervention and for formative and summative assessments.

Figure 1.1 An investigation: musical instruments

- *Wheels* The teacher's plans were for science work on the concepts of forces and friction. The basis for the term's on-going display was a length of muslin quickly and effectively decorated with tyre prints. This was done by stretching it out in the playground and rolling along it a collection of old tyres which had been passed through trays of paint. A second long drape on the theme of wheels was quickly made for the wall behind by tie-dye, using marbles and rubber bands. Against this background a sequence of on-going investigations was displayed. During the first phase children mounted different sequences of cog-wheels on blocks of wood, with accompanying quizzes for each other about which colour wheel would turn which and in which direction. Another on-going investigation involved huge pulleys fixed to the rafters by a parent, who was a builder. These were used to investigate the forces needed to lift things.

  The next sequence of investigations focused on friction. The children created a series of different surfaces inside cardboard box lids: gravel, grass, mud, sand and plain cardboard. A toy tractor attached to a piece of string with a spring balance on the end could pull weights across the different surfaces to measure the force required.

  This led on to a final sequence of experiments, in which children designed and made their own buggies and measured the force needed to move them in Newtons. A visitor, finding a huddle of little girls sitting on the step with a ramp apparently idly running toy cars down it during lunch time asked what they were doing. 'We're forming a hypothesis' she was told.

  At the end of the term's work some children decided to cut up the display drapes printed with tyres and wheels to make cloth covers for their topic books.

  The teacher had planned the content she intended to teach during the term. This was a cross-curricular topic, focused on a local farm, to investigate why it had not flourished or expanded before the days of mechanization. The scientific concepts she planned to teach were force and friction; the ideas for the investigations had come through discussion with the children. They were reflected in the physical, social and intellectual classroom environment throughout the term.

Other examples of on-going aesthetically presented investigative displays to which children can return individually in spare moments at lunch or play-times and also discuss periodically as a class include:

- *Making sets of objects* In hoops, jars or boxes, to explore concepts devised by themselves or selected by the teacher (big/little; heavy/light; transparent/opaque, colour groupings, phonic groupings).

- *Carding, spinning, weaving* An area where children can card fleece, spin wool and weave small decorative pieces on hand-made looms. In such on-going and therapeutic activities children can work both individually and collaboratively and learn from each other, for short or long periods. (This display stemmed from a visit to a reconstructed Iron Age village).

● *Patchwork* A corner where children can design and make small patchwork squares for a collaborative project. This began with class mathematics lessons on measurement, angles and tessellation and resulted in a large cushion for the reading corner.

Collaborative painting, environments, models

Here children worked collaboratively, in response to a shared stimulus, to create an environment which then led to further enquiry.

Painting

● *The Trojan Horse* A huge collaborative painting which filled the wall of the reading corner. The horse was coloured quite quickly by sponge prints, then individual children painted themselves onto the picture as Greeks

Figure 1.2
After a lesson (at the National Portrait Gallery) on the Van Dyke painting of Charles I, children decided to make a collaborative copy; this was used as a basis for quiz questions for other children who had not been to the gallery. To write the questions children reviewed, discussed and extended what they had learned

Figure 1.4 A presentation: a museum of Ancient Greece
After a visit to the British Museum (as part of work on Ancient Greece) the children used corrugated card to create their own museum, to display drawings of artefacts seen in the museum, and to provide explanations and inferential labels for visitors

Figure 1.5 A role play area: a post office
This Key Stage 1 display stemmed from children's existing experience of their locality, their local postman, and letters and cards. This was extended by a visit to the local post and sorting office, and a visit from a postman who lent them his uniform, bag and bicycle. As the work evolved it included even and odd numbers, stories, letter and card writing, parcel-making including shape, conservation, weight and money, and story reading and writing. This was all part of informal play by the children, extended into more formal situations by the teacher

Figure 1.7 Storage of resources
Storage of resources (paper, fabrics, wools, embroidery threads) which is aesthetically satisfying and allows children to make sensitive and informed choices for which they are responsible

Figure 2.3 Creating the background of the Hadrian's Wall display

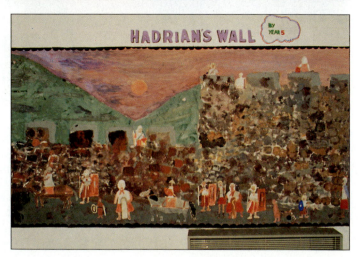

Figure 2.5 The finished display

Figure 3.4 Getting Dressed
Fishermoss Primary School, Portlethen, Aberdeen, Class Teacher: Mrs Avril Sloane. An example of 'loose-fit' in display, where children can contribute and respond meaningfully at any level

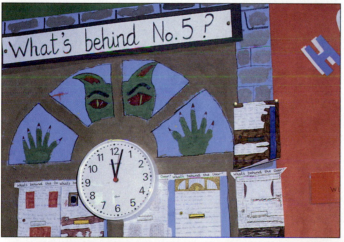

Figure 3.5 What is behind Number 5
Fishermoss Primary School, Portlethen, Aberdeen, Class Teacher: Mrs Avril Sloane. An example of 'a high-demand display which requires real engagement by the learner

Figure 3.9 Autumn
Grange CE Primary School, Helen O'Neill (student teacher)

Figure 4.3 Arousing emotions can be achieved either explicitly or implicitly

Figure 4.4 3-dimensional objects are represented 2-dimensionally by young children. The ability to perceive objects as 3-dimensional is an aspect of perceptual development which teachers can influence through display

Figure 4.6 Developing perceptual skills can be achieved by examining particular qualities of a picture and surmising the feelings of the artist (Taylor, 1986)

descending from the horse. This was done in response to hearing the story and was used as a stimulus for further reading of the Greek myths and legends displayed in the reading area.

- *Charles I* (Figure 1.2, p.28) This followed a lesson on the Van Dyke portrait in the National Gallery. It was painted on the floor on paper divided into twelve A1 sections and involved discussion, skills in colour matching and observation of historical detail. It was used as the basis for a quiz about the portrait, using information the children had learned on their visit to the National Gallery. Answers to the questions were concealed under flaps beneath the painting.

- *Greek vases* Following a visit to the British Museum slides of Greek vase paintings were projected on paper as very large images and painted. This is quick, effective and accurate as it involves only two colours. The results were stunning and were used as the basis for both formal enquiry and guessing games and as focus for further reading. Alternatively children can make their own drawings on overhead projector film.

Figure 1.3 Creating an environment; a Stuart Room
After a lesson in the Stuart Room at the Geffrye Museum children created their own Stuart Room by projecting two slides of the room onto screens in a corner of the classroom, then drawing and painting them. A borrowed costume added period detail. The room was used as a basis for further research about furniture, artefacts and costume, which informed both informal role play and story-writing as well as replica lessons for children who had not visited the museum

Environments

- *A replica room* (Figure 1.3) After a visit to the Geffrye Museum, where each room is furnished with artefacts and furniture from a particular period, children projected two slides of the Stuart Room onto two large screens which formed a right angle in a corner; they painted the projected pictures and so created a 'Stuart Room'. A costume was borrowed from a local dramatic group and displayed on a stand in the corner. Children could then show visitors around the Stuart Room using the information they had learned in the museum visit and extended during class lessons. They could share what they had learned and had the time, the 'aide-memoire' and the incentive to ask questions and research further. This was another excellent opportunity to store what is learned, draw on it, contest it and extend it in new contexts.

- *The wood* After a visit to the wood behind the school, where children identified, photographed and drew trees, plants and birds, a corner of a large open-plan unit was transformed into a woodland glade. Leaf rubbings from identified trees was suspended on nets from the rafters; plants were meticulously painted; animals known to exist in this habitat (although not observed) were researched and added; and explanatory labels were written. This led to correspondence with a local farmer about the care of the wood, a visit from a conservation group and a letter to the borough council. Within the teacher's selected focus – the local wood – and the concepts and skills she planned to teach, which were concerned with finding out about 'living things and the processes of life', decisions and momentum came from the children in the class and from the questions and ideas of other children in the open-plan unit. Similar shared areas have been developed on rain forests.

- *Imaginary places* Another successful idea was the creation, through class discussion, of an imaginary place in order to discuss a topical issue, for example whether an unspoiled beach in a poor community should be converted by a property developer into a tourist attraction. Children researched what the place might look like, and created it on the classroom walls, (sponge prints or paint rollers cover large areas very quickly and props such as fish nets can be added as available). They discussed who the various groups of inhabitants might be and how they might live and work; then each created a role, a family and a perspective for themselves. They painted their own houses and this led to a debate on the issue in the village square and a community decision.

Models

- *A timber frame barn.* As part of the science work on forces children visited a farm to compare the materials and structure of a timber barn and a new steel, concrete and fibreglass building. They then constructed roof trusses of different designs using straws, and met as a class to test them by balancing them between two tables with a weight on the cross-beam of each roof truss to see whose was the strongest. The competitive element is always motivating. On the basis of this competition, over a period of time groups of children constructed a rigid 'timber-frame barn' from rolled and taped newspaper that was large enough to stand inside. This was their own idea and the subject of continuing experiment and discussion.

- *A doll's house* An example of a collaborative Key Stage 1 model was a doll's house made out of cardboard boxes, complete with electric lights, burglar alarms and door bell. The teacher's aim was that the children develop some technological skills and learn about electric circuits. They decided in groups on what furniture and electrical appliances to make for each room in *their* house, which became the focus of extended free play and story writing.

Presentations

There are many contexts in which the classroom environment can be developed in order to present investigations to an audience of other children, or parents and interested visitors:

- *A classroom museum* This can involve research, inferences, explanatory labels, brochures and quizzes.
- *A local study* The teacher had planned a local history study in which children would work in groups to investigate changes in the history of four key buildings. The children decided how their investigations would be presented to local residents at a tea-party at the end of the project. This involved an illustrated talk and a map of the area on which listed places lit up when appropriate buttons were pressed, a model of the church from which taped music emerged accompanied by a tape-recorded history at the press of a button, and a computer controlled model of the railway which had been the cause of the main changes in the village.
- *Museum of Ancient Greece* (Figure 1.4, p.29) Steps were created from staging blocks, pillars were made of rolled corrugated card and a card pediment was decorated with Greek motifs. These were quickly made by photocopying and enlarging motifs from a British Museum booklet. The 'museum' was used to display, describe and explain drawings of artefacts in the British Museum (which had inspired the school replica). Further research led to an information booklet for visitors.
- *The haunted house* This Year 6 classroom environment was created by a very demanding class as part of a term long science and technology project. When it was finished children from other classes were invited (for a small

fee for charity) into the darkened room, where skeletons sprang up, the touch of a button caused strange noises, bats swung across the room, and spiders' rose and fell above their webs.

- *Interactive displays based on story themes* (Key Stage 1) *The Very Hungry Caterpillar* (Eric Carle): a child can crawl through the holes as the story line is read or recited. *Threadbare* (Mike Inkpen): a pulley can get Threadbare up the chimney as children read the story. This caused much delight and interest, especially from the children who had not been directly involved in the work associated with it.

Role play areas

There is no single all-embracing theory of play and no general agreement on the role of the teacher in initiating and supporting it. However all theorists have recognized the importance of different aspects of play – social, emotional, physical, intellectual, exploratory, action-motivated, imaginative and problem-solving – in the learning process. Yet one HMI survey (DES, 1989) found that the educational purposes of play for young children are often not fully understood or catered for. For older children the potential for planning and assessing learning through play across the curriculum is almost totally ignored. Hall and Abbott (1991) suggest that for all ages the National Curriculum has put too great an importance on the outcomes of children's learning rather than on the process.

Piaget (1951, 1954) regarded young children as mainly isolated individual learners, who build their schema through experiences in play and apply the accretion of new knowledge and skills to their play. Vygotsky placed more importance on learning through collaborative play with children and adults using each other as a resource and learning from each others' experiences. Bruner suggested that children learn through a combination of free and directed play, in which the teacher structures and scaffolds the child's development and experiences.

Moyles (1981) has to a large extent resolved the extrinsic/intrinsic free play/directed play dichotomies. A teacher may help to initiate a play situation through which planned learning intentions across the curriculum can be achieved. In Moyle's model, through initial free play, children explore, internalize and assimilate those aspects of what they have learned and experienced which are meaningful to them. The teacher intervenes to redirect and extend this understanding, thus requiring children to accommodate new information. In this way the accretion of knowledge and skills continues as a spiral. Such play is enjoyable and motivating. It enables children to initiate their own learning, starting from their existing knowledge and conceptual understanding; it is therefore matched to their individual abilities. This enables children to revise and practise situations which they are ready to respond to at a higher level, and so develop confidence. Such play involves language, social interaction and self-discipline.

The following are examples of role play areas which children can be helped to create for themselves as a basis for free play, and in which the teacher can later intervene to extend learning, involve a variety of curriculum areas.

At Key Stage 1:

- *A desert island* (Treasure maps, shells, paper sea, fish, palm trees). Reception children were seen sitting in 'boats', sailing towards the island, pretending to be pirates. The voices they used were those of true pirates and their language was far more advanced than they were thought capable of. The technology exercise, making palm trees, involved problems of balance. The children counted the fish they caught and designed symbols for the treasure maps.
- *A space ship* Children selected and classified materials to use such as shiny materials for space suits. They made a board of clock faces, buttons and dials for timing and count down. There was a great deal of rich imaginative rhyming language as the space-ship took-off.
- *Variety of shops* (Toy shops, supermarkets, sweet shops, hairdressers). These gave the children confidence to recognize and be able to read names on familiar wrappers, packets and posters. This confidence lead them to make lists of customers' preferences, name badges, notices showing opening and closing times, till receipts and bills.
- *Other places familiar to children* (A baby clinic, a hospital, a children's library, a bus). All offered children opportunities for number, reading, writing, listening, technology and plans.
- *A post office* (Figure 1.5, p.29) This, complete with postman's uniform, bicycle and letter bag, created opportunities for drawing familiar routes on maps, ordering house numbers, making cards and writing letters, sorting, using dates, consulting times of collections, money calculations, making 3-D parcels, weighing, visiting the Post Office, and inviting the postman into school to be involved in the play.

At Key Stage 2:

- *A cave* (Figure 1.6) Part of a history topic on the Stone Age, this involved projecting slides of cave-paintings onto paper on the wall and painting them with pottery oxides; designing and making weapons out of wood, flint and leather pieces (bows and arrows, spears, slings); testing them on the field, under strict supervision; recording graphically the distances across which each could be thrown; ritualistic hunting dances and dramatic

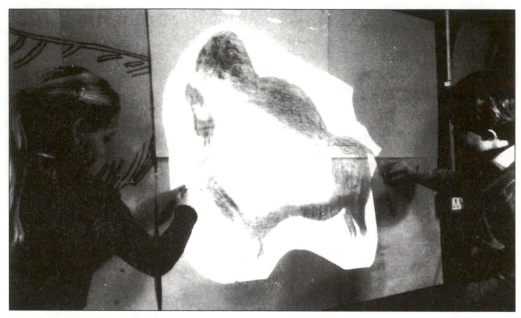

Figure 1.6 A role play area: a cave
Oxides were used to reproduce Lascaux cave paintings after a visit to a local cave where there was evidence of Stone Age Settlements. The paintings were projected onto the walls. Creation of the cave involved designing and making weapons from plant, wood and leather scraps, and replica neolithic pots. Informal play over a long period led to story-writing and drama and to an assembly presentation examining concepts of fear and of power, now and in neolithic times

play based on hunting which were eventually performed for an audience; sorting plants collected on a visit to the site of a Stone Age settlement into plants for bedding, medicinal plants, food plants; observational drawings of plants, and making pots based on neolithic designs, decorated with twigs and feather imprints.

- *A travel agency* This was part of a Year 6 geography project and arose entirely from the children's ideas. A piece of net curtained off the corner of the room. Children installed the computer for making booking forms, collected and displayed travel brochures, and made a series of leaflets on such matters as how to telephone home from abroad. This involved some demanding work on understanding time zones which was supported by the teacher, and considerable research about local climates, food and transport in order to respond to customers' questions. It also required complicated money calculations to advise customers of the cost of different hotel and travel options and much consultation of maps to find out where places were and what they were like.

Although all the geography and mathematics content, concepts and skills had been built into the aims of the teacher's scheme of work for that half term she had no intention of teaching it in this way. However she was able to support and direct the children's ideas and intervene in the organization to ensure that everyone was involved and that they all achieved some work she could use to assess what they had learned.

THE NEED FOR A WHOLE SCHOOL POLICY ON MANAGING THE LEARNING ENVIRONMENT

The importance of whole school policies in defining shared aims to which all members of teaching and support staff contribute, are articulate about and work together to implement, is now generally recognized. Shared philosophy and expertise create consistency, quality and the possibilities of development. A school policy on display and the learning environment needs to be underpinned by a clear statement of philosophy. It is the argument of this book that this should be firmly based on constructivist theories of how children learn; learning begins with what each child already knows, understands and brings to bear on a new area of study. Learning occurs through interaction between children and their environment both individually and collaboratively; this is initiated, supported and extended by skilled intervention from the teacher. In this way existing knowledge and conceptual understanding are consolidated, extended, challenged and recognized. The learning environments which are created in school must reflect this process. This philosophy has implications for planning, curriculum organization, classroom organization, and the organization of space and resources.

Planning

Teachers' medium term plans need to show clearly the content and concepts to be taught. There need to be suggestions within this framework for the ways in which, through interaction with the classroom environment, children may be helped to explore new knowledge, experience and concepts. There also must be flexibility for children to devise their own ways of doing this. Through this process teachers can create opportunities to assess what children initially know and understand, and to review with them what they have learned at the end of a unit of study (see Table 1.1, p.15).

Curriculum organization

There are implications for curriculum organization. If children are to learn in holistic ways and be responsible for their learning within a broad framework of aims, teachers need to be flexible and confident enough to recognize, record and exploit the learning which is taking place, possibly incidentally, and maybe in curriculum areas not initially planned for. For example, language development, technology, science, maths, music and art may arise within a history focused topic.

Classroom organization

There are implications for organizing groupings within the classroom; clearly there needs to be some agreement about turn-taking, timetabling and expected learning outcomes if all the children in a class are involved in creating a role-play area or making a collaborative painting, in fabric printing, in making a model or in an on-going investigation. Alternatively if not all the children are to be involved what degree of choice is possible and how are different children's experiences to be recorded?

Space and resources

A whole-school policy needs to state why it is important for children to learn the skills and techniques of trimming, mounting, book-making and displaying their own work; the aesthetic judgement, independence, responsibility and ownership involved. It is essential that the value of such skills and judgements is understood because the processes take time to learn. A whole-school policy needs to agree and justify a consistent approach to the skills and techniques to be learned throughout the school and to show how these are to be progressively learned. They may for example be taught to interested parents, who teach them to children in small groups giving children increasing independence, or children may help each other, older children helping younger children, in a 'cascade model'.

If children are to be encouraged to develop such independence there are implications for the ways in which resources are sorted, so that children are encouraged to make considered and sensitive choices. For example, if wools, fabrics, threads, beads, papers are sorted into categories and stored so that subtle and enticing gradations of tone and texture are on permanent display, not only does this contribute to the aesthetic quality of the environment, but it also encourages children to make considered and sensitive decisions about precisely which shade of green best matches a particular leaf vein or which combination of mounting papers best enhances their picture, which type of brush or paint or glue meets a particular need and which medium best suits a given purpose (Figure 1.7, p.30).

Similar decisions are involved if children select their own equipment for a science or mathematics investigation or a musical composition. Children are making affective, aesthetic and intellectual choices about the ways in which they respond to their world, which will be transferred beyond the classroom.

Finally the whole-school policy needs to take into account not just the classroom environment, but also the use of space throughout the school both indoors and outside. Can shared working areas be created for specific purposes (for cooking, for discussion, pottery or fabric printing), where groups of children can be supported by the more experienced adults, not necessarily their teachers, or where cross-age phase groups can help each other to develop new skills? How can areas outdoors be developed to enhance learning across the curriculum (an adventure playground, a pet area, a garden or wild area), where children can be supported by each other and by adults in taking considerable responsibility for maintenance, and which can be used as an inspiration and learning resource?

There also needs to be a considered policy for the kinds of artefacts and furniture which form the basis of the school environment. Should the barriers between school as an institution and the outside world be deliberately blurred, and if so how and why? In one school, for example, there is a cooking area where children in groups, throughout the school, take it in turns to prepare a meal, in keeping with the themes of their work – a Victorian or West Indian recipe, for example – and invite a guest of their choice to share it with them. The dining room furniture is deliberately conventional, bought from a local store. Similarly the discussion areas are furnished with carpets, lighting and lounge furniture discarded by parents. A book press is an old French traditional press acquired by the headteacher, and plant containers are made by ceramics students at a local college. Prints and paintings are of the highest quality. Does this not put out messages about the nature of the educational process in which children are involved? Student teachers, when asked these questions, have rejected such possibilities as 'cloud-cuckoo land', but they can and do exist, where teachers are sufficiently confident, inspired and committed to create them.

It is to be hoped that students will see such aspirations as part of their longer term aims for professional development. Newly qualified teachers are expected to have a basic understanding of how children learn, of the various factors which affect this process, to be able to create a purposeful and supportive learning environment, and to use a variety of strategies to teach children individually, in groups and as a class. If they also possess vision, imagination and critical awareness, they can continue to develop their expertise in all of these areas throughout their careers, to create classroom environments which are increasingly complex, sensitive and sophisticated.

2

Whose Work Is It Anyway? display in a negotiated classroom

Neil Simco

Whatever the content and nature of a classroom display, it is a significant reflection of that classroom. Display is a public statement of the beliefs about teaching and learning a particular teacher holds. It follows that there are a number of views about the purpose and function of display. One view is that an attractive presentation of children's work is a celebration of the work; display in this sense is essentially an end product of what has been achieved. Another view is that it should be an integral part of the learning which children experience. For example a teacher puts up questions as a starting point for further discussion and new activities, arranges a number of objects and artefacts which children can talk and write about and draw, or regularly changes the display to reflect the extent of the work already done and the new directions the work may take. A third view is that displays can represent the various ways in which children work in primary classrooms: the class as a whole, groups within a class, or as individuals.

These views have one thing in common, namely an underlying assumption that it is the teacher who controls the display, including both the actual work involved and its arrangement as part of the classroom environment. A good deal of classroom work leading to the production of displays reflects this assumption. Although these ways of thinking about display are important and valid, there are questions which need to be asked. For example, 'What are the consequences of putting the locus of control with the teacher? Does transferring ownership to the children lead to a greater sense of learning, independence and responsibility?

This chapter considers these questions in a discussion of display which is based on a different assumption: that the children should have a substantial share in the creation of a display. They take the lead in deciding what they want displayed, how they want it displayed and then actually implement their decisions as they provide the work and the display itself. This is not to say that the teacher has no role at all, that the work leading to the display is totally child-centred. Rather it suggests that the teacher's role is to engage in a subtle process of negotiation, guiding, managing and overseeing the children during the production of the display. In the process, the teacher interacts with the children as a class, in groups and as individuals. This approach lends itself to a publicly recognised joint ownership of many aspects of classroom life, including the organisation of work, the allocation of time and the content. In short, the principle which underpins this approach is that display should reflect an ethos of negotiation between the teacher and the children and between children and children.

This chapter is in itself an example of collaborative work – an essay constructed and composed in a negotiated partnership – in much the same way as the classroom work that we go on to describe. The classroom teacher is my wife, Samantha Simco. At the time when I was exploring the concept of the negotiated classroom, Samantha agreed to keep a detailed record of work which she was undertaking with her class of Year 3, 4 and 5 children. This work was focused on a study of Hadrian's Wall and formed part of a wider topic on Roman Britain. During the weeks of the topic, and later, we were able to ponder, discuss and interpret her thinking-in-action – some hundreds of on-the-spot decisions – and later her reflection-on-action (Schön, 1987) – as we discussed the work and together analysed the components that we saw as integral in creating a negotiated classroom.

First I will review the work of the educational researchers who have shaped both my thinking and Samantha's work with her pupils. Ingram and Worrall's illustrative definition is a useful starting point (1993:3):

> The teacher has deliberately set up a classroom context to frame in the children's minds their responsibility as negotiative partners in their own learning experiences ... The teacher uses his knowledge of the children, the classroom resources and classroom language to move the children to a position of planning, reflection and self-organisation.

In this respect negotiation is about giving children a full and ongoing opportunity to contribute to the life of the classroom through shared ownership of significant aspects of that environment. The negotiated classroom is one where both teachers and children have this shared ownership of the events taking place in that classroom. This differs from what Ingram and Worrall term 'the conventional classroom' in so far as the teacher does not dominate classroom processes. The idea of the negotiated classroom has far-reaching consequences for the kind of teaching and learning which goes on there.

The notion has its origins, on one analysis, in two connected ideas. One approach to understanding the importance of the term is to link it with a view of the classroom as a complex and multi-layered place whose ethos is defined by the thousands of daily interactions which occur between teachers and pupils, and between pupils and pupils. The concept of negotiation is compatible with such a view because it consists of the meaning which is given to these interactions by the different participants, both children and adults. In short, one way of understanding the importance of negotiation is first to understand the complexity of classrooms.

The work of the American researcher Walter Doyle (1977) is particularly useful in providing a foundation for understanding the idea of classroom negotiation. Doyle sees himself as a classroom ecologist, asserting that the idea of the classroom as an ecology can be defined by considering a number of elements. (See Desforges and Cockburn, 1987 and Simco, 1995 for a full summary.) One of these is the notion that the classroom is naturalistic, in other words that classroom life is characterised by an intense complexity. Doyle (1986) goes on to explain that classrooms have a number of key attributes, including multi-dimensionality, simultaneity, unpredictability and publicness. Multi-dimensionality refers to the large number of events that occur in any classroom. Two children's conversation in one corner of the classroom might be deeply significant for their learning, whilst in another part of the room a solitary child is struggling to understand his work. Doyle also suggests that these events occur simultaneously, the consequence of such an assertion being that at any one time there will be a plethora of events that are significant for different classroom participants, teachers and children. It is perhaps because of multi-dimensionality and simultaneity that Doyle sees classrooms as being unpredictable: it is not possible for any classroom participant to predict the exact nature of the classroom process which will occur. Classrooms are public places as the teacher's and children's actions and reactions are in the public domain, belonging to all classroom participants. The Doyle view is that classrooms are places of naturalistic human behaviour in which the environment is significant in determining that behaviour. The environment, in turn, is defined by the actions of teachers and pupils in that environment.

Another way of understanding the origins of negotiation in classrooms is to link it with the theoretical concept of symbolic interactionism (Mead, 1934). This is a fundamental concept in social psychology; it is concerned with the creation of meaning between people, based on messages which they give to each other verbally and non-verbally. People act in ways that are determined by understandings gleaned from others. This position relates to the view that a person's actions and behaviour are not a product of genetic make-up but rather are occasioned by the multitude of interactions in which any individual participates. It is the opposite of saying that a person is born with a set of given attributes which determine the kind of person she or he will be. The person's social environment is an important determinant of their behaviour in that environment.

These ideas can be readily applied to classroom negotiation. Using Doyle's terms, the ecology of the classroom will be determined not by the genetic make-up of the individual participants, but rather by the social processes which occur as individuals relate to and interact with each other in the classroom. Thus it is possible to have a classroom which consists of a complex set of negotiations through which a consensus between the participants is defined.

This idea of the social environment in which certain acts and behaviours are exhibited can be clearly linked to the classroom negotiative processes which are described by Woods (1980). He suggests that one of the assumptions which underpins negotiation is that pupil-teacher relationships are created by interactive processes. Moreover, these processes are not created once and for all; rather, they are subject to constant modification and re-negotiation. Woods goes on to suggest that another assumption underpinning negotiation consists of the reality of power relationships in classrooms. Certainly in Ingram and Worall's terms the negotiated partnership is realised by a shift in power from the teacher to the pupils. Woods's final assumption is that teachers and pupils have different interests; the classroom is the arena in which these interests have to be catered for and acknowledged.

Having briefly outlined the origins of negotiation within both symbolic interactionism and the idea of the classroom as a complex ecosystem, it is now useful to consider the characteristics of negotiation as a central feature of classroom life. Pollard (1985:158) provides a useful framework for such an exploration. He classifies a number of strategies which teachers use in order to develop what he terms the 'working consensus' in the classroom. This is seen as 'the idea of teachers and children mutually negotiating interdependent ways of coping in classrooms'. Pollard goes on to contrast different strategies which pupils and teachers might use. He suggests that domination on the part of the teacher will lead to rebellion by pupils. In this way pupils and teachers act unilaterally: there is no consensus. At the other end of the spectrum is what he calls 'open negotiation' – the mutual accommodation and respect of the interests of both teachers and children. Within these two extremes Pollard describes a range of negotiative strategies between mutual acceptance and domination/rebellion. Two examples are given. The first is the teacher's attempt to routinise classroom activity and the children's urge to drift from this routine. The second is concerned with the teacher who tries to manipulate classroom life, with the consequence that children try to evade what the teacher is endeavouring to achieve.

Other writers offer perspectives on negotiation within classrooms. Warham (1993) contrasts the teacher who tries to achieve power by dominating children with the teacher who endeavours to seek power by consent. Most strikingly however, Warham distinguishes between the different kinds of power relationships that a teacher might have with different children in the class.

Negotiation can hence be seen as operating on at least two levels. The first is concerned with broad negotiative processes with the whole class – arguably most significant in determining the overall ethos of the classroom because of the public nature of the actions and behaviour of the teacher and children. Domination or open negotiation are established clearly during the public exchange which constitutes the introduction of a lesson. This links closely with Doyle's assertion that the publicness of classrooms is an important determinant of their ecology. According to Warham, the second kind of power relationship that a teacher might have with a class is seen in the interactions with children during 'seatwork'. Again this idea can be related to Doyle's notion of the classroom as an ecology. It gives further expression to the idea of the classroom as multi-dimensional. It is misleading to say that a teacher has only one kind of power relationship with the children in her class. However, because of the publicness of whole class introductions and interventions, it is probably valid to say that this is the most important in establishing the overall ethos of the classroom.

In appraising the role of negotiation, a useful starting point is the view that negotiation is an important part of classroom life, if teachers and children are to survive. This perspective is hinted at by Pollard when he suggests that the working consensus is about serving the needs and interests of both teachers and pupils. It has even greater expression in Peter Woods's work; he presents a view of the classroom where the dominant motive for teachers and children is survival, towards which end all participants adopt a range of strategies and approaches that serve their interests. Woods (1990:vii) suggests that schools 'are places of struggle, where teachers and pupils do their best to cope with the problems set up where social constraint collides with personal intention. The result of this struggle can lead to happiness or misery or the combination of the two'. Whilst this kind of perspective is a legitimate interpretation of the role of negotiation and consensus in classroom life, it can to some extent be seen as a deficit model. It seems to suggest that negotiation arises out of the need for survival rather than the desire to be creative and cooperative. Negotiation is portrayed as negative rather than positive.

Another perspective acknowledges the role of negotiation as survival but places greater emphasis on the benefits of negotiation for the creation of an ethos in which both pupil and teacher interests are realised through a productive and creative environment in which all participants can achieve success. Ingram and Worrall (1993:14) state that:

> We were concerned about how many children brought to the classroom interests, motivation, curiosity, knowledge and ideas that our conventional teaching behaviours somehow failed to nurture – and in many cases de-powered and de-valued. The attraction of negotiated partnership grew ... from a feeling of unease and unhappiness with the conventional relationship of teacher and pupil.

This perspective is echoed elsewhere. Ainscow and Tweddle (1988), writing about children with Special Educational Needs, state that negotiation between teachers and pupils is essential if children are to achieve the kind of success which fulfils their potential. Hart (1992) sees that the collaborative classroom, achieved through effective negotiation between classroom participants, is an important factor in ensuring children's cognitive and affective development.

Linking these two perspectives, it is important to acknowledge the roots of negotiation in the need for teachers and children to survive in classrooms, the existence of different points of view being part of the human experience. It is perhaps equally important that the negotiative process is not seen merely as a coping strategy for classroom conflict resolution. To do this denies the power of negotiation to transform the learning experience of children so that they have a fuller say in both the content and the organisation of their work. As will be seen from Samantha's account, such an approach has the potential to lead to richness in children's learning.

THE CLASSROOM

It is now time to invite you into the classroom as Samantha and the children continue their topic on Roman Britain. We have captured their progress in words and photographs and divided that record into a number of scenes so that readers can step back, as we did, and place the action in the context of our thinking on the negotiated classroom. Samantha takes up the story:

I teach in a village school in south Cumbria. The school is organized into three classes and, at the time of the work we discuss here, I had been teaching there for two years. I knew the children and they knew me and my way of working. There were 28 children, fairly evenly divided over Years 3, 4 and 5.

The class had been studying 'Romans in Britain' for some weeks and had already investigated the Roman invasion and the Celtic resistance. We were about to begin a study of different aspects of Roman Society.

All the children sat around me on the carpet as I explained the division of the work: Roman roads for Year 3, Roman baths for Year 4 and Hadrian's Wall for Year 5. I had collected some reference books on Hadrian's Wall as a starting point for the Year 5s. I gave them 45 minutes to browse through the books (Figure 2.1). I had designed a simple record sheet so that they could record the key points along with enough detail so that the information could be located quickly later in the project. We then listened to a radio programme designed to be used with the topic. When the presenter asked questions I encouraged the children to think about the information they had just been reading.

At the end of the programme I stated that their project was to make a display on the theme of Hadrian's Wall. I outlined the criteria for this display – that it should be interesting, attractive and informative. The children began to shout out their ideas but I told them that they would be presenting and discussing these ideas on

Figure 2.1 Gathering information for the Hadrian's Wall display

their own in the next session and then we would meet together to discuss what they had in mind. I left to work with Years 3 and 4.

When I came back to the Year 5s I listened quietly for a short time as they went on with their discussion and then I asked them to tell me what they had decided. This was to create one big picture with labels, based on a rough sketch. Each of them would submit a sketch and the final choice would be made by vote. I was uneasy about the voting procedure and its subtext of winners and losers. To get around this I said that the vote would only be for the basic design; the details would come from everyone.

I circulated around the tables as the children worked, asking questions that would challenge them to think more carefully about the project: Where would the labels go? Should there be people? Might a different perspective other than 'head on' be possible? I also reminded them that most of the illustrations they had seen were of the wall as it is today, whereas their job was to create a picture of the wall in Roman times.

When the children came together to vote, there was a tie. I intervened at this point to initiate a discussion about the two designs in relation to the criteria I had set out earlier, that the final display should be informative, interesting, accurate and include labels. Following this discussion one design was chosen and the children decided that all would contribute and that new ideas could be incorporated as the work proceeded (Figure 2.2).

At the next meeting of the group they began to draw a rough version of the eventual display. There was lots of talk and discussion. Disagreements were

Figure 2.2 Developing a group consensus

usually settled by consensus and compromise although sometimes they resorted to voting, as they had done when deciding on the general shape of the display.

When the children invited me to look at their final draft design I raised some issues, particularly about the display of textual information. Although I suggested some possibilities, I continued to leave the decisions to them.

The development of the display took place over several sessions. On the first day two children prepared the background paper, laid it out on the floor of the school hall and began together to draw the outline of the rough sketch. I stayed in the classroom to work with Years 3 and 4. When the outline was finished they asked me to advise them on how to obtain a 3-D effect. It was now ready to be painted. One child suggested using sponge painting for the sky. Four children went ahead with the sky while the other four started on the wall (Figure 2.3, p.30).

With the background finished, discussion turned to the foreground and the soldiers and horses. The children decided to use the reference books for ideas and began on rough sketches. Further discussion resulted in the decision to have two horses and fifteen soldiers and the children began to transfer their rough sketches into their final form. Differences in the size of the figures provided the lead-in for me to raise the question of scale and proportion; the children decided that the figures and horses should be the same size.

Although I wanted the children to have lots of time for decision-making and work, we still needed a plan to ensure that the display would be completed in the time I had allocated for the project. I talked this over with them and then with each child individually. At this point each child agreed the work to be done and

Figure 2.4 Finishing touches: mounting the display

a completion date.

The final phase was the mounting of the display on the board (Figure 2.4). On discovering that it needed to be trimmed the children thought the best way was to cut off the top. I realised that this would spoil the completed work and persuaded them that artistically it might be better to trim a little from both top and bottom. The remaining work – a border and the title – were undertaken by individual children.

Parallel with the drawing and painting, the children had discussed the textual information that would accompany the display. Several children wrote drafts. The agreed version was largely taken from one child's draft with additions from others. They selected the child with the neatest handwriting to produce the final document.

Combining the elements proved difficult and the children were clearly unhappy as the display moved towards completion but still did not live up to their expectations. I suggested that using a ruler would be helpful for completing the lettering, and the display now came to resemble more closely what they had envisaged. When it was finished the children were clearly proud of their achievement (Figure 2.5, p.30).

I wanted the children to undertake a piece of reflective writing about the whole process of creating the display. We talked about the kinds of questions that would be useful to frame and extend this reflection and I wrote the questions on the board, at the same time encouraging them to go beyond the outline questions which were:

- Are you pleased with the the finished work: why?
- What are you most pleased with: why?
- What could you have done better: how?
- What were you like as a group member?
- What have you learned from doing the display?
- Anything else?

As part of this work, each of the year groups made a presentation to the class.

In one sense this is a typical primary classroom. There are three groups, grouped in this case according to age. There is a common class topic and each group is making a contribution in different ways. There is one teacher who has the responsibility for managing the class, achieving a delicate balance between facilitating learning and direct instruction. There is a busy but controlled working environment with all the children fully involved in what they are doing. Visitors would see a happy, busy place with children working enthusiastically. They would possibly go away with a common sense perception that the process of teaching and learning is straightforward and unproblematic.

As this chapter seeks to demonstrate, this perspective denies the huge complexity of the task of teaching. Looking at the scene much more closely, it is possible to see the consequences that the actions of all the classroom participants (both teacher and children) have for the success of that teaching and learning.

During her introduction to the topic, Samantha managed to gain and hold the attention of the group of children whilst also maintaining an orderly atmosphere in the class as a whole. This was possible because she kept the pace of the explanation moving, a task which in itself involves perhaps tens of professional decisions about speed of exposition, when to ask questions, how to monitor the rest of the activity in the classroom, and how to respond to the child who wants to intervene in the midst of teacher explanation. The management of this introduction is critically important because both teacher and children are setting the scene for the task ahead. This goes far deeper than the content – it is concerned with the way in which the project is to be carried out.

A significant moment was Samantha's handling of the last couple of minutes of the introduction when the children were shouting out ideas and suggestions. Initially the children tried to use their teacher as a respondent for their ideas; they were looking for her approval. The whole pattern of interaction was for the children to suggest, the teacher to respond and the children to proceed according to this response. The children did not talk to each other but were immersed in trying to find out what the teacher thought was important. It seemed that they wanted to have little ownership and take little responsibility for the task. They wanted to be dependent on the teacher who would effectively decide for them the content of the display.

Samantha's agenda was different. She wanted them to have ownership of the display, to be independent and yet to be responsible to each other for the work which they undertook. She adopted this approach because she believed that the quality of the outcome was directly related to the degree of ownership which the children had over the work. She wanted the children to feel secure about making decisions about their work before any interaction on her part and to be confident in sharing their ideas.

A situation may develop where the children want the security of final decisions made by the teacher, whilst she wants to encourage and support risk-taking and collective responsibility.

A negotiated classroom is not merely dialogue between teachers and children. It is concerned with more subtle patterns of interaction and management. Samantha managed to negotiate with the children so that they ended up in a position where they were prepared to take risks and to work together. She showed the children that whilst she was not prepared to answer their questions, she was prepared to set up a framework, the circle, for them to come to their own decisions.

Circle time is one of Samantha's key strategies. The physical arrangement of children in a circle is a powerful way to establish a negotiative ethos. At the common sense level it might seem that small changes in physical arrangements have a negligible effect on children's experiences. In Samantha's classroom the creation and use of a circle of children was indicative of all that she wanted to achieve with her pupils. That the children moved so readily in and out of this format during the creation of the display meant that they too saw the value which this had in promoting a classroom in which the opinion and view of each participant was seen to be of value.

Normally circle time is defined as a gathering of teacher and children where the teacher plays the leading role in the management of the time, inviting children to speak or allowing child-child dialogue to develop across the circle. In Samantha's version, there were different kinds of circle time. Some of the time was similar to this definition, but the spontaneous move into a circle with the children taking on the key role was different.

This observation can in turn be related to some of the key questions which Housego and Burns (1994) ask about the concept. Firstly, they ask whether circle time fits in with the particular classroom ethos, suggesting that if the classroom is characterised by domination rather than negotiation then the idea of circle time is likely to be redundant. In Samantha's classroom, as has already been suggested, the pattern of intervention, placing much emphasis on the elicitation of children's ideas before any teacher intervention, is indicative of a rich classroom culture. In addition, it has already been demonstrated that she skilfully handled the beginning of the display work so that a negotiative ethos was established in which the children had substantial but not total ownership of the work. It is as a consequence of the consistency and perseverance of the negotiative climate, that circle time flourished in the project in the way that it did.

The second question which Housego and Burns ask is whether the content of the circle time is superficial. They go on to cite an occasion whereby the teacher asked the children to list their favourite activities. The children in turn announced their activity, uttering their response as a one word answer. The writers also suggest that the content of circle time might be less satisfactory if the teacher is only prepared to accept different children's contributions with interest and respect, rather than to challenge their thinking and ideas. Because of the necessity to spend this time with the other year groups, Samantha has had to establish a framework that will support the children when they are left on their own. Because of careful preparation over a period of several months, the children are skilled at asking questions of each other and jointly agreeing an outcome.

That the children were already skilled in asking questions had positive outcomes in terms of the end of the work. Here Samantha encouraged them to evaluate their work by first compiling a list of questions. The process through which the questions were decided was compatible with the idea that the classroom had shared ownership between teacher and children. As the questions were constructed neither teacher nor children had dominance in their definition. They were explored and debated in dialogue and then Samantha wrote them down for the children to use as a framework for their reflections. The questions were not to constrain the children's responses but rather to allow them to emphasise aspects of their work which they considered to be important. The children's evaluations on p.58 emphasise this point. The first one has a focus on the actual content of the display whilst the second is more about the group work which was necessary in order to produce the result.

Another key strategy is intervention, particularly its timing and form. For example, when the children are deciding how to tackle the display task which they have been doing, Samantha comes into the circle at one point but chooses not to intervene at all. The next intervention comes when she refines the children's approach to taking the vote, suggesting that they might undertake a secret ballot. Later she challenges individual children on aspects of their work. These three examples are important because they are different to prevailing patterns of intervention found in many classrooms. In the first place there is no interference at all. Samantha merely listens to what the children are saying so that she can understand the purpose of the children's

independent negotiations. A more conventional approach would have been
to leave the children to talk about the display and then to intervene, asking
them about what decisions had been made and why they had been made.
The children's response to Samantha is also interesting in that they carried on
with their deliberations and did not appear to be affected by her presence
thereby accepting the role of the teacher as an onlooker. This is indicative of
the subtlety of the relationship between the children and the teacher since it
might normally be expected that the teacher's presence would have an effect
on the children's behaviour. The children are confident that they have the
ownership of their discussions and that they have a degree of autonomy in
fulfilling their goal. This has not happened by accident but is the outcome of
what Hart (1992) calls the collaborative classroom. The whole ethos of the
classroom created over several months is concerned with children
confidently working with each other and respecting each other's views and
opinions. Successful non-intervention could not have occurred if this pattern
of collaboration had not been present.

Had Samantha intervened at this point , the children's embryonic
discussions and ideas might well have been crushed and turned into
something which reflected the teacher's mind rather than what was in their
minds. That the children felt free to continue with their discussions was
reflective of the whole ethos of the classroom. It is only when the children feel
secure in their deliberations that Samantha intervenes; she does so in order to
challenge the learning which is going on. Here she decides to suggest the
secret ballot in order to protect the self-esteem of children whose work might
not be selected, and to ensure that children vote according to their assessment
of others' work rather than according to friendship loyalties. There is also
intervention with individual children as their ideas are challenged in respect
to the criteria for the project and an opportunity to justify their individual
point of view. Again these challenges are subtle as the children are not told to
provide labels for the display in a certain way. They are asked whether this is
something which they should consider and if so how?

The pattern of Samantha's intervention illuminates aspects of what Silcock
(1993, 1994) terms 'new progressivism.' This idea is also expressed by Galton
(1989, 1995) who uses the phrase a 'redefined version of progressivism'
(1989:130). This view arises out of the notion that neither the traditional nor
the progressive paradigms are completely successful in providing a useful
description of what occurs in classrooms. Classrooms are no more places of
didactic instruction and rote learning than they are of free discovery. Silcock
(1994) suggests that pupils need skills for independent learning and that
these skills can only develop in a classroom climate where 'learning is seen
as a joint enterprise between teachers and children' (1994:5). Both Galton
and Silcock imply that it is necessary to redefine progressivism to

acknowledge the complexities of classroom life and the real existence of negotiation. Galton (1989:131) describes one aspect of this as the negotiated approach where

> the teachers' interventions are kept to a minimum until pupils are sufficiently confident in the value of their ideas to admit publicly to ownership. Once this stage has been reached, the pupils will no longer try to hand back control of the learning to the teacher by feigning dependency... Once pupils have accepted 'public ownership' of their ideas, the teacher can act as critic rather than judge in ways that many teachers often find difficult because as we have seen, children interpret the teacher's evaluations as personal rejection and so lose self-confidence.

Samantha begins by giving the children space and time to develop their own ideas and to feel confident about exposing them to the public arena of the classroom. Only at this point, when the ideas are sufficiently strong and well formulated, is she prepared to intervene and this is done in such a way that it enhances the children's confidence in what they are doing through the use of carefully placed questions.

It is interesting to note that the research agenda over the last decade or more has had a substantial focus on the questions that teachers ask of children. Clearly this is an important aspect of classroom life as teachers will find it necessary to ask a great many questions every day as part of their work. The description of the work which went into the Hadrian's Wall display is rather different. Here is an example of a negotiated classroom whereby the ownership of the work is brought into the public domain. This has implications for the kind of questions which are framed. Naturally some of these questions will be from the teacher to the children, as when Samantha challenges individual children about aspects of the work which they are doing as the display is created. However, central questions like the evaluation of the display itself (see p.58) are a result of negotiation by teacher and children. They are not framed by one individual participant in the class, either teacher or child, but every individual has freedom to respond in ways which they think appropriate. Public definition and ownership does not in this way deny the individual child freedom to respond as he or she wishes.

This contrasts with Wragg's (1993) study of over a thousand teachers. He found that 8% of teachers' questions were of a higher order in that they involved more than data recall, whereas 35% were of a lower order, involving only information and data recall. Fifty-seven per cent were of a managerial nature. This kind of pattern may or may not have been reflected in Samantha's class. The important thing is that the central questions which drove important parts of the Hadrian's Wall display were higher order and had shared ownership. They asked Why? and How? and were constructed jointly by the teacher and the children.

In looking at Samantha's classroom in a systematic way, it has been possible to gain some insight into the detail of the teaching and learning processes which occurred as the Hadrian's Wall work was displayed. It is worthwhile to look at the description as a whole from this perspective. What kinds of things can be gleaned from the account about the overall approach which Samantha has to her teaching, and the role which the display has in reflecting these aims? One framework which is particularly helpful in exploring this is provided by Rowland (1987). He proposes that there are three models of teaching and learning processes which can be used to illuminate both the importance and the difficulty of the negotiated model which underpins the particular approach to display which is considered in this chapter.

Rowland firstly cites what he calls a *didactic model*. In this model, it is the teacher who sets the scene by defining the needs of the pupils. The pupil then responds to this initial stimulus and the teacher in turn marks the pupils' work, responding with further instruction. Rowland believes this to be the dominant model, suggesting that

> ...even in the most favourable circumstances of teaching a single child to play the piano, under no pressure of time, or space, it is very difficult not to teach in a didactic manner. After all, I have the knowledge and the skill. Isn't my task to transfer this knowledge and skill to the child? Am I not the one who knows best which activities will promote these abilities? (129)

It is easy to see how display can be a public statement of this model. The teacher controls the initial stimulus, the children's response and the eventual outcome. The display is thus highly likely to be a product of the children's understanding of what the teacher wants rather than a joint teacher–pupil expression of the classroom activity. The didactic model is definitely not one which is adopted by Samantha.

This is contrasted with Rowland's *exploratory model* in which the child has almost full responsibility for the work. Here the initial stimulus is negotiated between the teacher and the children, but it is the children who take up this stimulus and who respond with minimal teacher intervention until the end of the task when the teacher intervenes. The locus of control is with the child. Again classroom display could be a public expression of this approach. The display would show the results of children's work without any critical intervention from the teacher. Despite the words and phrases widely used to describe such an approach – discovery, enabling, facilitating – this approach arguably lacks opportunity for critical reflection and perceptive challenge, being altogether too open. Samantha's classroom is not compatible with such an approach. The display which emerges at the end of the work cannot be described as belonging totally to the children. It was they who did all the work, including the eventual erection of the end product, but it was the teacher who was prepared to intervene in ways that both stimulated the children's thinking about what they were doing, and, perhaps more importantly, encouraged the children to debate classroom events.

Samantha's approach is perhaps best reflected in Rowland's third model which he calls the *interpretive model*. Here an initial stimulus could come from either teacher or a child. It is, however, important that the child has ownership over how the stimulus is interpreted into what is actually done. The teacher then acts as reflective agent, clarifying what the child is doing and acting as a critical friend to that child. In response to addressing problems and issues, the child will invent and as a result of this she or he will be able to identify skills and knowledge which are needed to fulfil the invention. At this point the teacher might intervene to offer instruction which the child can then apply to the needs which have been highlighted.

In a sense the learning processes through which these children went were more complex still because of the way in which they worked with each other. It seems that the children were not merely responding to each other as they developed the display, but that at times they took the role of reflective agent. This is entirely compatible with the negotiative classroom because it means that the boundaries between teacher and learner are blurred. Samantha has successfully enabled the learners to take on the kinds of roles which are normally reserved for the teacher. Taking this on board, it is possible to adapt the Rowland model so that it takes into account occasions when the child takes on the role of the teacher.

If any model is to have use then it is important that it is influential in changing actual practice. Hence it seems appropriate to end with a professional challenge. This chapter set out to demonstrate the processes involved in helping children to work towards and produce a display which upheld various principles. These are:

- Display is a public and prominent statement of the teaching and learning which goes on in the classroom.
- It therefore reflects closely the nature of the central teaching and learning processes which are defined in that classroom.
- It is worthwhile exploring teaching approaches which are about shared ownership between teachers and children, having the potential for children to take responsibility and develop independence of thought.
- Negotiation between children, and between teachers and children, will be important if shared ownership is to become a reality.
- The extent to which negotiation is expressed is determined by the fine-grain aspects of classroom life, such as the way that the teacher handles

questions, the approaches that are used for intervention in children's activities and the use of appropriate managerial strategies such as circle time.

● If a negotiated classroom is to become a reality then close attention must be paid to the way these fine-grain issues are dealt with.

A professional challenge arises from these principles. At the very beginning of the chapter, there was a brief attempt to outline the kind of classroom processes which lead to the creation of display. It was suggested that many of these approaches, perhaps even when the work itself has an element of shared ownership, can serve to undermine the benefits that can accrue from celebrating a real negotiative classroom. If it is the teacher or the child who is at the centre of the production of a display, then a very clear message is being given about the values which are explicit in the classroom. If display is created in such a way that there is full opportunity for negotiation and shared public ownership, then this has the potential to develop the key attributes of responsibility and independence. As has been seen from Samantha's classroom, this is not a panacea for 'discovery'; rather it facilitates a classroom ethos where advice and constructive criticism can be offered by different classroom participants, thereby contributing positively to the self-esteem of children. In a negotiated classroom, children can feel secure in their learning.

The notion of a negotiated classroom is not, of course, concerned only with the creation of display; it will permeate many aspects of classroom life. But display is important because in one sense it is the public record of the work of the classroom. It reflects the values and attitudes held by both teacher and children and situates the locus of control within the classroom. The professional challenge is to consider the range of possible approaches in the production and display of children's work and, within this, to facilitate a negotiated display.

Since this chapter has been about the work of a particular group of children, it seems appropriate to let them have the last word, in the shape of two of their evaluations of the process of creating their display:

> I am really pleased with the result that we came up with. It looks good on the wall. I especially like Hadrian's Wall because it has got a lot of detail. It was a real achievement for me and Year 5. I have learnt more about Hadrian's Wall and the mile castles and the forts. To work in a group you have to cooperate and be fair and let other people do things.

> I am really pleased with our results of Hadrian's Wall because I think the sunset is brilliant and I like the way we've done the wall with sponges. I am most pleased with the sunset because I like the nice purply colours we have used. As a group member I think I could have been better but it is harder being in a group

than working on your own. I've learnt that by being in a group you have to cooperate and I've learnt a lot about Hadrian's Wall. If you keep working you will get it done and have an excellent result.

3

Quality on Display: tasks, learning and the classroom

Phil Hegarty

What is display for? Who is it for? What makes a display 'good'? This chapter aims to shed light on these questions by taking the ideas and methods of general task analysis and using them to analyse particular classroom displays. First then, an overview of task analysis and the theories and principles it draws on.

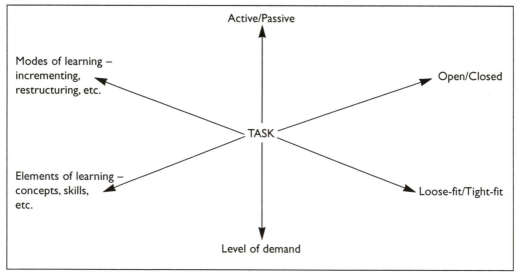

Figure 3.1 Perspectives on task analysis

One way of analysing tasks is to consider the role of the learner as positioned on a continuum between active and passive. Children as active participants in their education was a theory at the heart of the Plowden Report (DES 1967). Notions such as the child as 'the agent of his own learning' and 'finding out is better than being told' were treated as axiomatic. These related principles became litmus tests of good practice in the child-centred and progressive education movements and remain, for many teachers, reference points for quality. Clearly, these ideas can be used to evaluate display, particularly in respect of the children's involvement and ownership.

Another way of analysing tasks is to consider how open or closed they are – that is, to what extent the learner is free to determine the processes, outcomes and levels of difficulty. Thus, some tasks are heavily teacher-directed, often with precise intended learning outcomes and leave little scope for the children to adapt or modify the task to their own interests or level. Others are starting points, usually with ways of proceeding and end-points suggested but with deliberate provision for choice, decision-making and ownership. Display can be used to serve both kinds of task but the nature and style of display will be very different.

The notion of the fit of task and learner is a related idea. Tasks which are loose-fit allow the children to find an appropriate level of demand for themselves; tight-fit tasks are structured and focused on a particular learning outcome at a particular level. As with the open-closed dimension, the roles of teacher and children shift markedly according to whether tasks are intended as loose-fit or tight-fit, and the functions of display, too, are different. Again, direction and ownership are key issues. In loose-fit tasks, there is scope for children's influence; in tight-fit tasks the teacher is central.

Using level of demand in task analysis is perhaps best explored in Doyle's work (1983). He proposes a typology which sorts tasks as memory, procedural/routine, comprehension/understanding and opinion and links these to the idea of low- and high-level demands. Low-level are dependent and highly teacher-structured tasks, high-level require real engagement by the learner. Choice, ownership and responsibility are key ideas.

Another familiar way of thinking about tasks is to consider the elements of learning they are intended to facilitate – concepts, skills, knowledge, processes, attitudes and values. It is obvious that, for example, a display intended to impart knowledge would be very different from one designed to support or report children's explorations or investigations. Different again would be a display focused on attitudes or values.

Finally, the influential work of Bennett *et al.* (1984) has given us a task typology which links directly to modes of learning – incrementing, restructuring, enriching, practising and revising. The central idea here is that the process of acquiring new learning depends on a sequence of modes and overlapping stages. Again, these ideas have a strong purchase on display. For example, a display might be designed to support and structure the learner's first encounter with an idea, concept or process or it might be designed to suggest, provoke or report investigations or problem-solving.

These ideas provide a set of frameworks which allow us to analyse and assess the value and power of tasks in supporting learning. Two sets of ideas are embedded in them; these might loosely be described as cognitive and affective. Thus, there are ideas which relate to levels and kind of intellectual demand, kind of cognitive process and so on. Then there are ideas which relate to children's feelings about the task. These two sets of ideas were nicely juxtaposed in a model proposed by Bloom (1976). Here the key idea is that what children bring to every task can be described as a set of cognitive qualities and a set of affective qualities; what they take away are changes in cognitive qualities and changes in affective qualities. The affective element – that is the expectations of success or failure, confidence or fear, interest or boredom and so on, that the children bring to each task and are modified by each task – is of course, not separate from the cognitive; the two affect each other. That there must be a dynamic between them can be illustrated by focusing on match as a determinant of children's responses to tasks. What happens when children are assigned tasks which are manifestly beyond their reach? Or when a child is confused by the teacher's explanations and instructions? The affective response is, then, closely linked to the cognitive.

If we accept that there is a dynamic relationship between the cognitive and the affective in children's response to tasks, then we need to pay attention to processes as well as to content. Raths (1971:716) proposed that a task is better, or more worthwhile, if:

- children are permitted to make informed choices;
- children are assigned active roles;
- children are asked to engage in inquiry;
- children are involved with real objects, materials and artefacts;
- it can be successfully completed by children at several different levels of ability;
- it asks children to examine, in a new setting, an idea, an application of an intellectual process, or a current problem which has been previously studied;
- it requires children to examine topics or issues not usually studied;
- children and teachers are involved in risk-taking;
- it requires children to re-write, rehearse and polish their initial efforts;
- it involves children in the application and mastering of meaningful rules, standards or disciplines;
- it gives children the opportunity to share the planning, the implementation and the results of an activity with others;
- it is relevant to the expressed purpose of the children.

We have touched on a wide-ranging and complex set of ideas which are helpful in general task analysis. Key ideas which are useful in linking task and quality can be summarised as clarity of purpose, fitness for purpose, openness, match level and meaning, choices and reflection on choice, responsibility and ownership, and safe risk-taking, confidence and self-esteem.

How can these ideas be used to structure our thinking about display?

First a caveat. It is easy to make quick and uninformed judgements on brief classroom visits when there is no opportunity to discuss the history, learning context and purposes of the displays. In an infant classroom with children ranging in age from four to seven the kinds of work and involvement will clearly vary. A set of nursery rhymes with the outlines and faces drawn by an adult hand provide the opportunity for the youngest (perhaps with the help of the older ones) to fill in the outlines with a variety of materials. The labels have been printed by the teacher since these young children do not yet have the skills for this part of the public display. But further questions might be raised about the involvement of the children, their ownership and the ways in which the displays support the children's learning.

We all have pictures in our mind of 'good' classroom display. There is one that I recall vividly. As I walked through the door I had to crouch to make my way under a rain forest canopy, ingeniously suspended from the ceiling.

A profusion of greenery, animals, insects and birds were closely woven into or suspended from nylon garden netting. Around the room was a series of more formal displays, some obviously the work of the teacher, some clearly the work of the children. Most were informative, describing in words and illustrations the variety of life in the rainforest, food chains, ecosystems. Posters exhorted the reader to save the rainforest. There were wallbooks made by groups of children, each written to a theme. The immediate appeal of this classroom needs no further description. It is exciting to enter, it's fun, interesting and informative. It relates clearly to ongoing current work in the class. Many of the objects have been created by the children, much of the work had been structured and presented by them. The children's enthusiasm and sense of pride in this achievement were evident as they told me about their rainforest. Now this isn't an unusual example. The creation of a themed environment, the extent of children's involvement and a sense of pride and achievement can be found in classrooms everywhere. But why is it good? Is it because it looks and feels interesting, because of the children's involvement and ownership – or more?

In order to make sense of such generalised and intuitive responses to display we need to find ways of analysing – thinking frameworks which we might use to clarify responses and, more importantly, support our planning for display in our classrooms. This chapter now returns to the task analysis ideas introduced earlier.

Passive/active

A.C.F. Beales, in his paper 'The historical development of "activity" methods' (1955), traced those 'methods' back to Socrates, and on to St Thomas Aquinas who, in the thirteenth century, illuminated the benefits of an active approach to teaching and learning. He formulated the case for treating the child as the active agent of his own learning in terms of the nature of the child, the kind of adult who emerges and the ideal under which teacher and child work. Active approaches are held to be appropriate to the flexible nature of the child's mind, to build the characteristics which lead to balance and confidence in the adult, and to support an ideal relationship between teacher and learner.

There are many resonances between the ideas of Aquinas (and later progressives such as Pestalozzi, Froebel and Dewey) and the modern progressivism expressed by Rowlands (1987), Galton (1989, 1995) and Silcock (1993, 1994). Although still an emergent philosophy of education, modern progressivism can be defined by its concern with method and outcome. Interpretive methods which engage the child with real thinking and meaning-making are proposed as effective. The outcomes – independence, self-reliance, confidence and collaborativeness – are held to be indispensable in the development of responsible citizenship. The concern is with methods and with overarching goals.

The value of using the active-passive dimension in display analysis lies in its simplicity. It is easy to ask the question 'Are the children receiving information from the teacher or are they, in some way, actively involved – operating on the information, exploring, discovering, trying out, making sense?' This question allows us to differentiate that which is instruction from that which engages the children in their own learning. It is when we attempt to evaluate the activity that the question becomes complex and difficult as we meet the need to analyse the purposefulness and effectiveness of activity and to distinguish between mere activity and that which is efficient and effective. In modern progressivism, activity is focused not so much on the 'what' of tasks, but on the 'how'. It is the development of methods by which children engage with problem-solving and the discourse which informs and evaluates the methods which makes it 'modern' or 'new' progressivism.

What has all this to do with display? Just as with tasks, we can start with the question, 'What is the role of the children here?' This is not to encourage hasty judgements. There is an important place for display that brightens a dull hallway or welcomes visitors at the school entrance. Individual displays need to be considered within the context of the whole school. I recall a school entrance decorated with huge daffodils and the children's poems and stories mounted at eye level, an integral part of the whole. All of this might be dismissed as mere wallpaper, but conversation with the children might reveal their pride in transforming the hallway. Conversation with the teacher might reveal the ways in which undertaking the display allowed less able children to have an important part in creating a display that was remarked on by staff, children from other classes and visitors.

In another classroom (a high-ceilinged Victorian room), the children's writing is mounted almost touching the ceiling, impossible to read. A casual visitor might be appalled at this. But within the context of the class work, it is revealed as a brilliant teaching ploy.

The writing is about the earth in space, and children use a telescope to read their classmates' contributions – one of the very few times I have seen children reading each others' displayed writing. This display required an active response and, because of this, excited interest in both the use of the telescope and the content of the display. Other examples of displays which require or stimulate activity include displays that 'work', with flaps, levers, circuits and so on; those which excite a thinking response – questions, puzzles, etc.; and those to which children add contributions day by day. An example of a display that 'works' is shown in Figure 3.2 – the children's response to the problems posed in *The Lighthouse Keeper's Lunch* (Armitage, 1977).

Figure 3.2 The Lighthouse Keeper's Lunch
Fishermoss Primary School, Portlethen, Aberdeen, Class teacher: Miss Margaret Stokes.
A display that works – the children's response to The Lighthouse Keeper's Lunch.

However, the active–passive idea can be taken much further if we consider the links between task and display. In a sense, the two can be seen as inseparable. Where the task, or sequence of tasks, leads to a concrete product – text, illustrations, models, diagrams – there is always an opportunity for children, especially collaborating groups of children, to communicate their work in the form of a display. This is not to say that display should always, or even often, be the outcome, but it should be kept in mind as an option. The benefits relate to both the ethos of the classroom and to the process of the task. If the teacher aims to develop an ethos in which ownership, responsibility and collaboration are important and valued qualities, then the fact of children's real ownership of display can be a contributing factor. If a task or sequence of tasks can sensibly be communicated or reported to others in the form of a display, then the planning, design and production of the display can give purpose and meaning to the task, a context for the product and a very immediate reason for care and quality. Process and product are interwoven. To return to the active-passive idea, here is an example of the content of task, its process and its product being reflective of the principles of active learning.

To summarise, the active-passive idea might be used to analyse display in respect of the values expressed in the classroom environment and in respect of the linkages between task and display.

Open-closed

The notion of open–closed relates to two key ideas – the extent to which children have ownership of the ways tasks are carried out and the degree to which the task permits the child to find an appropriate level of demand. Thus, a task might be open – 'How can we tell the story of *The Very Hungry Caterpillar* in pictures', or closed – 'I want you to stick these circles together to make a picture of *The Very Hungry Caterpillar*'. A related idea is that of the clarity or vagueness of the task (Simco, 1995). Clearly, displays can be open or closed both in the processes which lead to their creation and in the messages which they convey. Similarly, vagueness or clarity are characteristics which might be observed in both the process and product of display.

The relationship between the open–closed and vague–clear dimensions are expressed by Simco (1995) in a model which he proposes as a tool for analysing activity (Figure 3.3).

			ACTIVITY	AMBIGUITY
A c t i v i t y A m b i g u i t y	D e g r e e o f C l a r i t y		Degree of Openness	
			Open	Closed
		V a g u e		
		C l e a r		

Figure 3.3 Neil Simco's model

The four cells in the matrix suggest four possibilities. For example, activity can be characterised as open and vague. This would apply where, for example, children were asked to record the outcomes of a science experiment, but there was little understanding of whys and whats of the experiment and the recording process. Or the activity might be characterised as closed and clear where the processes of experimenting and recording were preceded by clear instructions and then heavily directed and paced by the teacher, with little or no scope for children to own the activity. As a model for analysing tasks, this matrix has much to commend it; in its own terms it is clear and open, allowing the teacher to peel off layers of complexity when thinking about the underpinnings of their beliefs about quality in learning experiences.

The model is equally of value in analysing classroom display. This works at two levels. Firstly, it might be applied to the process of analysing a planned or existing display from the teacher's perspective. Secondly, it can be used to analyse the processes by which children and teachers together create a display – the tasks which end up being recorded in display.

Imagine a display of the once obligatory angels and snowflakes in an infant classroom at Christmas. The teacher's purposes are clear – to display work by every child and to create some seasonal decoration. The display is also closed in that there is nothing more to do with it or say about it. On the other hand, openness and clarity in a display might be characterised by questions embedded in it. For example, to continue the seasonal theme, a collection of foil parcels and decorations of different 3–D shapes might be linked to nets, some of which do relate the 3–D shapes and some of which don't, with scope for children to add more. An example of a display which is closed and vague might be a row of children's stories, mounted and pinned up. Displays which are carefully designed by the teacher to recall or reinforce a concept, a skill or factual information – for example sequenced portraits of the Tudor Monarchs or reminders of 'how to be a good response friend' to support shared writing – are clear and closed.

The implications for quality of display are not difficult to discern, although they should be used with care. The key question is 'what is the reason for the display?' Thinking about the purposes of a display can be supported by the linked notions of open/closed and vague/clear.

When applied to the analysis of tasks which relate or lead to display, the model is equally powerful. A project on the sea might include studies of life-forms, food-chains and ecosystems; a history of explorations and discovery; or a collection of poems and pictures. All of the strands of the project suggest display themes and ideas, but here lies a trap. If the curriculum planning process leaps from broad idea to display without considering tasks then display is likely to be an add-on; opportunities to integrate display into the task process will be overlooked. The opportunities for children to plan and execute display themselves have obvious merits in terms of developing design, planning and collaboration skills and maintaining a sense of ownership and responsibility; they also provide scope for the concepts, skills and content knowledge of the curriculum to be discussed and communicated by the children. Clarity and openness are crucial in linking tasks and display. The task might be to compare and contrast different poetic and visual interpretations of the sea. The initiation of the task would depend on the teacher's selection of materials, the clarity of explanation and the eliciting and discussion of key ideas. Openness would lie in the children's decision-making about how the comparing and contrasting could be represented. It is openness and clarity which matter. The resulting display may or may not exhibit the same qualities; it doesn't matter, as long as the evaluation of the display with the children is done properly.

To summarise: Simco's model, applied to display, can be used to analyse displays on open/closed and vague/clear dimensions. For teacher-provided displays, the key issue is the purpose of the display. The model can also be used to analyse the linking of tasks and display. Here, qualities of clarity and openness in the tasks are crucial.

Tight-fit/loose-fit

This aspect of task analysis relates to the match of task and learner or, more precisely, the degree of self-matching the task allows. When teachers plan tasks the question of level always comes into play: Will the children be able to do this? Will it be too easy? Newly qualified teachers often make the mistake of thinking that they always have to do the matching, which, on closer analysis, turns out to be impossible. No teacher can match tasks all day every day for 25 or 30 individuals. Who then, usually does the matching? The fact is that whether the teacher intends it or not, the children do the matching – either in response to a task which is deliberately left loose-fit, or by re-defining or re-negotiating the original expectations. Whilst some tasks, especially those involving new or incremental learning clearly need to be matched precisely, skilled teachers recognise the imperative of loose-fit qualities in most tasks, so that children can find their own level of demand and response. Quality depends significantly on the attitudes and feelings that the child brings to the task. Interest, motivation and confidence are crucial determinants of how well the task will work.

The notions of ownership and responsibility clearly have a purchase on this way of analysing tasks. In a sense, when a teacher designs a task as loose-fit she is relying on the children's attitudes and the ethos of her classroom to secure positive responses. Where children readily accept responsibility and ownership loose-fit works. When they don't – usually because of low interest, poor explanations or cultivated dependency – loose-fit doesn't work.

To summarise, then, loose-fit tasks are those where the level of response lies in the child's hands. This can also mean that the kind of response is also in the child's hands (see open-closed, p.66), but not necessarily.

To apply these ideas to display, we need to return to the central idea of match and think about the teacher-directed/teacher-produced and child-controlled elements of display differently. In teacher-directed display, the key question concerns meaning. Does the display have meaning for the children? Is it cognitively accessible? Does it challenge at an appropriate level? Criteria to think about include the choice of pictures, diagrams and models; the level of language used in labels and questions; the ease with which children can refer to the display to recall, check or reinforce their ideas and understandings. For example, in a display in a reception classroom about getting dressed, photographs and active elements such as a tie or giant shoe with laces to practice on might all be carefully determined by the teacher, who pays special attention to the meaning-making qualities for all the children in her class (Figure 3.4, p.31).

Here is an example of an ideal display which, although heavily structured by the teacher, has the loose-fit but which leaves plenty of scope for young children to make their own contributions – possibly in pictures, flowcharts or writing – and to play a part in discussing and deciding the final form of the display. Every child can respond at some level and in some way to the process of getting dressed and can contribute to some element of the display. It allows for the least able and least confident, and for the most able and most adventurous. An important point here is that the fit of the display is managed by the teacher: the loose-fit of the children's contribution is embedded in the tasks which led to the display.

To summarise: the idea of loose-fit/tight-fit can be used to analyse displays in terms of match. Thus, teacher-provided/directed elements of a display might be carefully planned to ensure meaning for all the children. The tasks which lead to the children's contributions might be loose-fit, i.e. designed so that children can contribute in a variety of ways and at a variety of levels, and with as much or as little structuring as each child is comfortable with. It is worth remembering that loose-fit is only a virtue in so far as it matches the cognitive and affective states of the children involved.

Level of demand

The ideas in this section are drawn from Doyle's (1983) notion of task types and the kinds of demands they make on the learner. Doyle defines tasks as : memory, procedural/routine, comprehension/understanding and opinion. He implies that tasks such as reproducing information from memory or following standardised procedures to do sums are low demand. High demand tasks (those which require real engagement from the learner) include selecting procedures to solve a problem, drawing inferences from given information, interpreting evidence and assembling or synthesising information and resources to generate a product. These ideas relate closely to the notion of match of task and learner but the link is not simple. It is important to remember that, for example, different memory tasks might be appropriate to a five-year-old or a fifteen-year-old but they would all be categorised as low demand. Similarly, the task of drawing inferences from given information can be designed to match any ability or age.

How, then, can the idea of level of demand be applied to classroom display? The notion of engagement is particularly relevant here. Some displays require little engagement, they simply tell, remind or decorate. A list of days or months falls into the low demand category. This is not to say that such elements of display are not useful. They are often vital reference points for children which remind them of sequences and spellings and thus support their learning tasks. However, it is possible to picture classrooms in which all displays are in Doyle's terms, low-level. Higher level displays demand more from the learner (Figure 3.5, p.31).

Similarly, work on the styles of different painters might be supported by a selection of prints (say of flowers or gardens) with the questions 'Who painted which picture?' and 'Why do you think that?' Support might be offered in terms of other clues related to techniques, or examples of other work by the same artists clearly labelled. The children would be required to engage with the display in order to make use of it. This example also illustrates the idea that display and task can, and usually should, be closely interwoven. This display would be of little value if it did not draw on work already done with the children or if it were not used in class discussion about the 'reading' of paintings. Nor would it be of continuing value if it were not regularly updated, perhaps by the children

Displays that have working parts provide another illustration of high level demand. For example, levers and pivots or sets of cogs can be set up together with questions which ask children to predict 'what will happen if ... ?' and to design other mechanisms which will achieve a given outcome. Again, the key feature is that of engagement. The display requires a response and the children have to think in order to respond.

To summarise: the ideas of low-demand and high-demand can be used to analyse displays for both purpose and quality. Low-demand displays have their place, especially in reminding and supplementing children's use of newly acquired learning. High-demand displays require active engagement from the children.

Elements of learning

The elements of learning can be defined as concepts, skills, knowledge, processes and attitudes/values. Teaching approaches and tasks can usefully be analysed in terms of their appropriateness for the intended element of learning. For example, the related concepts of change and cause might be addressed in a science project on growth. Here, the children's ideas about the changes that take place when plants grow would be trawled to find out what their conceptual understandings were. Questions might be raised which could be investigated. Misconceptions would certainly be identified. Knowledge and gaps in knowledge would be uncovered. Children might or might not have acquired the skills they need to engage in investigation; they might or might not have the personal qualities and attitudes which support individual or collaborative study. The initial discussion reveals, to the skilled teacher, the concepts, skills, knowledge, understandings of process, and attitudes and values the children bring to the topic. The learning experiences are planned accordingly. The quality of the tasks will depend fundamentally on how well they are matched to what the children have already learned. Understanding the elements of learning will help the teacher to decide what kinds of tasks are most appropriate for the intended lesson and for these particular children. Thus, the development of children's concepts of change and cause might be supported alongside their skills of observation and recording by a series of tasks based on growing seeds or photographs of themselves at different ages. The development of knowledge – for example the conditions of successful growth in plants or humans – might be drawn from discussion and experiment. The importance of care and nurture might be addressed with the children's attitudes and values in mind. The central point is that clear thinking about the elements of intended learning helps the teacher to plan appropriate tasks. Can the same thing be said about display? Can the elements of learning be used as one idea to support the analysis of display? Should display, like tasks, differ according to what element of learning is intended?

Concepts

Take the example of the water-cycle. It does seem likely that a visual representation of this concept is helpful in supporting the child's understanding. Likewise, the concept of ecosystem could be illustrated in a way which makes the connections clear. Obviously, learners differ in the extent to which they find models and other forms of visual illustration helpful, but it does seem likely that these kinds of display have their place.

Knowledge

The ways in which display might support the learning of knowledge seem obvious. Knowledge of the Tudor monarchs, the life-cycle of the frog or the phases of the Industrial Revolution might be readily represented in ways which support children's acquisition of knowledge. But there is a danger here. The obvious way is for teachers to gather interesting materials and structure them into a display which informs – a finished and usable display. However, the value of such a display, its relevance and use by the children, might be much greater if it were an on-going display in which children were responsible for designing and making contributions.

Skills

Displays designed to support the learning of skills could also, at first sight, be seen as essentially teacher-provided. Skills commonly taught at Key Stages 1 and 2 include communication, observation, studying, problem-solving, numerical, and personal and social.

Rules or ways of proceeding for all of these are often displayed both as explanation and reminder. There is certainly a place for these displays, but the pedagogical benefits are increased if the children are engaged in deciding how to represent and explain the skills.

Processes

Processes can be thought of as the sequences or combinations of acts necessary to complete complex tasks. They involve concepts, knowledge and skills. The children might be concerned with understanding and explaining the process of generating and supplying electricity or designing and carrying out an investigation. Displays are most useful here in their capacity as media for children to explain and record – as a concrete end-point for a series of investigative tasks.

Attitudes/Values

Finally, attitudes and values are possibly the most readily observable link between display and the elements of learning. We need to consider the hidden curriculum in order to explain and understand this. Expectations of reliability, sociability, self-reliance, confidence, tolerance, initiative and self-discipline are expressed in the ways children and teachers work together, in the style of tasks and in the learning environment. Thus, whilst a code of behaviour might be expressed in displays, it is in the overall feel of a classroom that we find the clues to the link between display and attitudes and values. The two salient features are the aesthetic quality of the environment and the extent to which a sense of children's involvement and ownership is evident. The rain-forest display described earlier illustrates this.

To summarise, the elements of learning provide one way of clarifying our thinking about what it is we want children to learn. This classification has implications for display; different elements of learning suggest different kinds of display and different ways of using display to support learning.

Modes in the learning process

In 1984 Bennett and his colleagues published their seminal work on the match of task and child. The most powerful contribution of this work is the adaptation of Norman's model of schematic learning to produce a typology of tasks: incremental, restructuring, enrichment, practice and revision. Their research indicated that incremental and practice tasks tend to dominate leaving crucial modes of learning unsupported. The key idea here is that children need to be involved in all the task types in order to engage successfully with new learning and to use, apply, practice and revise it. Restructuring and enrichment tasks require the child to be active and creative. They involve discovery, invention, construction, problem-solving and application.

How does display relate to Bennett's five task types? The incremental phase (meeting a new idea, process or concept) can be supported by visual images such as models and pictures – anything that illustrates, explores, helps to make sense of the new learning. Teacher-provided elements of display are clearly of value. It is in connection with restructuring and enrichment tasks that children's display might have a particular part to play through providing a medium or context for both activity and communication. Let's take an example. In a unit on electricity, children often play with batteries, wires, switches and bulbs. Whether preceded or followed by instructions or explanations, children usually discover the fact that the circuit needs to be completed. The playing which precedes or follows this discovery is, in Bennett's terms, a restructuring task. What happens next – the planning and making of different more complex circuits, the design of lighting for a dolls house, the invention of different switching mechanisms are problem-solving and applications – are, in Bennett's terms, enrichment tasks. Here, the opportunities for task and display to be linked are obvious and manifold. Practice and revision might be best achieved by adding to and continuing use of the finished display:

- incremental (meeting new concepts, processes, skills) might best be supported by teacher-provided elements: diagrams, flow-charts, pictures, questions.
- restructuring (discovery, intervention, construction) might best be supported by teacher-provided elements which pose questions such as 'Which of these circuits would work?' 'What would happen if ...?'
- enrichment (problem-solving, applications) might be seen as using display

as an ideal medium for children to record and communicate their explanations. Children might show how they solved a circuit problem such as lighting a doll's house or create problems for others to solve.

- practice (becoming confident and slick) might link to display through children recording now familiar circuits and problems for others to use.
- revision (insuring against the decay of learning) seems to be best achieved through the continued use of finished displays, in which the teacher-provided and child-created elements are referred to in discussion and related to other new work.

To summarise, Bennet's task typology provides an analytical framework which we can use to ensure that all the key learning modes are considered when displays are planned. Thus, the learning purposes of display and the ways in which display might be used to enhance and support particular learning processes can be differentiated and clarified.

Task analysis, other perspectives and thinking about teaching

So far in this chapter, some perspectives from the literature on task analysis have been used to generate ways of thinking about displays. It is important to remember that these are analytical tools, not rules for practice. They are intended to support the process of reflection on practice. It would be ironic if any of the theories or ideas explored here were used to set rules for practice. Educational theory is not for creating rules or recipes for practice; rather, it is for providing ways to think about teaching.

Fenstermacher (1980) proposed three ways to bridge research and practice: with rules, with evidence, with schemata. Bridging with rules might be

Figure 3.6 Spiders: *Settle CP School, Class Teacher: Mrs Karen Robinson* – a story based display.

thought of as the antithesis of professional thinking; merely using research or theory to drive decision-making is not to be classed as professional thought. Using evidence, however, is. But perhaps the best way of using research evidence and theory is to treat them as a rich source of ideas, propositions and discourse which professionals can use to extend and elaborate their thinking about practice. None of the frameworks for reflecting about display are for the generation of rules, but they do contain evidence and, more importantly, a rich vein of thinking tools. Sometimes, none of the task analysis frameworks will be appropriate, as is illustrated by the story-based display in Figure 3.6.

But we might look elsewhere for yet another way of thinking about display. Display should always prompt one of three questions: What is it? Whose is it? Isn't it ... strange, amazing, horrible ... ?

Regardless of the framework used, the important issues are thinking professionally and remaining aware of the power of reflection on practice.

REAL CHILDREN, REAL TEACHERS

Using these ideas and the models (Figure 3.7) and criteria (Figure 3.8), Helen O'Neill, a student teacher now describes and reflects on her work with children in Mrs Jo Murdoch's Reception Class.

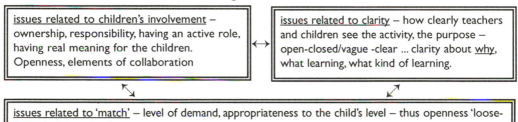

Figure 3.7 Issues in assessing displays

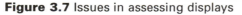

> What do the children think of the display?
> How often do they look at it/use it?
> What purpose does the display serve (e.g. in terms of learning, developing self-esteem, sense of ownership of the classroom, contributing to the visual appeal of the classroom...?

Figure 3.8 Criteria for assessing displays

This display grew out of some initial work with the children on the term topic of seasons. Naturally we homed in on autumn: we read stories and information books together, wrote a class poem and went for walks through the school grounds. My original idea was to create a table display for the interesting things the children were collecting on these walks. This led to the idea of a wall display and in fact work on both went on in parallel.

Among other things the children collected conkers, acorns, fir cones and sycamore seeds. They also involved children in other classes in looking for 'autumn things'. The display kept on growing. I made labels for each object and left paper, pencils and magnifying glasses on the table to encourage close observational drawings. I also took photographs on the walks and the children surprised me with their attention to detail, often pointing out things I had missed. One child was particularly delighted to show me a ladybird in the corner of one of the photographs

The main display had a border made of leaves, dried and pressed and glued onto a black background. I made an outline of a large tree, the children sponge painted it in various shades of brown, sprinkled on sand to suggest bark and rolled up newspapers to make 3-D branches. The leafy ground was a collage of autumn colours (also sponge painted) with an emphasis on the colours that the children had observed and talked about during our walks. I cut a template for the hedgehogs and the children came up with a number of ideas of what to use for the spikes – leaves, straw, sycamore wings, dried grass, hand prints. The badgers, mice and squirrels on the ground and in the trees were the children's own paintings which they made after a class discussion about autumn animals (Figure 3.9, p.31).

The children's individual work – observational drawings, stories, poems – was displayed around the room. I had the children fill a box with leaves and then made a lid with a small hole. This was the Scrunchy Box. Each child had a turn to put in a hand and describe how the leaves felt. I wrote their words on leaf shaped cards and glued them to the box.

The children were very proud of their displays and often talked about them and added to them. The displays became a focus and stimulus for the topic on weather and seasons, and their interest and involvement continued throughout the term.

I wanted to continue the theme of the seasons and the children agreed. Because of the busy excitement of Christmas preparations I hoped they would choose winter but in our brainstorming session on 'What winter means' Christmas won hands down. So we learnt Christmas songs and read winter poems.

Whereas the autumn display had one complete scene, the winter display was a series of scenes. Apart from making the templates for Father Christmas and the reindeer, it was the children's work (Figure 3.10). The border was snowflakes and the autumn tree was transformed to a winter one with cotton wool and the children's paintings of winter animals. There were five snowmen paintings (several children decided on this after learning a snowman song). We continued to improvise 3-D effects. The snowy ground was scrunched newspaper covered with a white sheet. The children collected twigs for the reindeer's antlers and built a sledge for Father Christmas out of boxes.

We also had a house with a Christmas tree and a fireplace. On the mantel the children arranged their handmade cards. The fire was a collage of coloured paper sprinkled with glitter and twigs. Paper chains, curtains for the windows, the children's mounted paintings, stories, and poems added to the festivity of the house. We also created ceiling mobiles for the classroom – angels, stars and robins.

Figure 3.10 Winter – *Grange CE Primary School, Helen O'Neil (student teacher)*

The making of the display helped the children to focus their pre-Christmas excitement, but it also helped them to notice and think about the changes in the woods as the year moved from autumn to winter.

My teacher-tutor, Mrs Jo Murdoch, decided to continue using similar display work through the spring and summer terms.

Purposefulness and clarity, ownership and involvement, match and level are generative concepts, useful in planning and analysing display work – but in a flexible and open way, driven not by rules but by informed reflection.

There are, though, ways of structuring reflection which support the process. A reflective thinking checklist could be part of this support :

- What is the display for?
- In what ways will it support learning?
- Is it the best way of achieving the purposes?
- Has it got an element of openness?
- Is it pitched at a level that is meaningful for all the children?
- Can it be produced in part or wholly by the children?
- Will the process of producing the display support the children's level of responsibility, confidence, collaboration and risk-taking?

Questions such as these can maintain the dynamics of continuity between task and display and as part of the expression of thinking and teaching.

4

A Child's-eye View: the development of children's perceptual skills through display

Penny Hegarty

It might be argued that display is a unique feature of classroom life in that the children are, largely, both creators and consumers – most of the work is produced by the children and it is displayed for their benefit. However, how can teachers ensure that children *do* benefit from display, apart from enjoyment of bright and cheerful surroundings? Do children give display more than passing attention? Do they appreciate their work when it is displayed – or, once finished, are they ready to put it behind them and move on to something else?

These questions inform this chapter in various ways, but my central concern is to explore the development of perceptual skills. I have used the work of developmental psychologists and educational theorists to evolve a framework for creating and analysing display that both incorporates and extends that development.

'Perception' is a concept that continues to engage psychologists and educational theorists. The notion of 'selective attention' is particularly relevant, not a simple intuitive awareness but the result of interest, focus and learning.

All of us take in information through our senses and organise that information to make meaning. Successful display stimulates in a way which encourages children to use their perceptual skills to further their knowledge and understanding. A brief review of studies exploring perceptual development indicates that, although all the senses are involved in perceptual development, the visual is probably the most powerful.

Fantz (1961, 1963) investigated what babies can see by showing pairs of patterns to babies between one and fifteen weeks of age. His hypothesis was that if the babies showed a preference for one pattern it indicated that they could see the patterns and discriminate between them. He found that the babies preferred the more complex patterns and would concentrate on these even if they were placed in different positions. Bower (1977) explored babies' responses to moving objects approaching their faces. Three situations were used: object movement with air movement, air movement alone and object movement alone. Air movement alone did not elicit any significant response but an object movement with and without air movement prompted a defensive response from the babies, including raising their hands in front of their faces. Babies' visual perception of faces has been shown to be particularly strong. Goren *et al.* (1975) found that newborn infants only nine minutes old can follow with their eyes a stimulus resembling a schematic face. Wertheimer (1961) found, whilst investigating the auditory perceptions of newborn, that it was possible to tell whether the babies knew where the sounds came from by the movement of their eyes towards the sound.

These studies appear to indicate that perception is an innate ability since newborn infants have not had the opportunity to learn. However, this nativist perspective is opposed by empiricists who believe that perception is developed through prior learning as children grow older. Cassells and Green (1991) propound Gibson's (1969) four perceptual strategies which, they argue, children employ from infancy to adolescence.

The first, *capture to activity*, indicates a 'general shift from scanning the environment in the hope that something will capture the attention' (Cassells and Green, 1991:32) to a more purposeful activity where intention and interest influence what is perceived. If the display is to have learning impact, children must be motivated and interested enough to actively engage with it. Pollard & Tann (1987) suggest three possible ways to stimulate children at the start of a session which could apply equally to stimulation through display. *Capitalizing on children's interests and experience* can be achieved through involving them in the planning and construction of the display, provided that the resulting display is not static, that it does not have an invisible 'don't touch me' label. *Challenging children to investigate* the display with opportunities for hands-on interaction (flaps, pulleys, levers, flashing lights, stop watches, feely-bags etc.) will also *channel their curiosity* to explore.

The way in which the display is perceived will become more complex as the children employ the second of Gibson's strategies, *less systematic to more systematic search*. Although infants study new objects carefully, recognition improves as children get older because they have previous experiences to draw on.

The appearance and formats of displays vary tremendously, from the fairly straightforward presentation of individual children's paintings to large collages filled with contributions from a number of children. The ability to focus on one aspect of a complicated situation is a perceptual skill which Gibson refers to as *broad to selective pick-up of information*. There appear to be two possibilities: the teacher can consciously establish a focal point to stimulate children's attention towards a specific area, or the display can be designed to encourage the children to identify a focal point important and relevant to them. In both cases vigilance at the planning stage is crucial, as is careful observation of children's responses when the display is in place and follow-up work is in progress.

Gibson's fourth strategy, *ignoring irrelevant information*, concerns the ability to ignore distractions. Cassells and Green (1991) liken this to the ability of students to concentrate when taking examinations in spite of extraneous noises. The notion that some aspects of a display might be irrelevant, however, is contentious. Many teachers assert that every element in a display is relevant otherwise it would not be there. However, the child who is not able to be selective in ignoring irrelevant information may be distracted by bright backgrounds or intricate borders and notice very little else. There also seems to be a case for some displays to contain just a few, carefully selected items presented for maximum impact (Figure 4.1).

Figure 4.1 Some children may be distracted if displays contain too many items. A few carefully selected items achieve maximum impact.

All four of Gibson's strategies are concerned with the increasingly sophisticated ways in which children organise the information they receive. Sylva and Lunt (1982) contend that most of the information received through the senses occurs through difference and changes in the environment, indicating perhaps that the length of time a display is in place before being replaced is another factor to be considered. There are obvious implications for use of the teacher's time when decisions are made about how often displays should be changed since creating worthwhile display is time-consuming. One solution is to develop an existing display, rather than replace it. This will sustain children's interest and attention and also reduce the amount of time needed from the teacher.

In a classroom where there are many displays of different sizes, shapes and types children need the opportunity to discriminate, select and learn from those aspects which are most useful and relevant for them. What is perceived by any individual is a function of perceptual set, 'a perceptual bias or predisposition or readiness to perceive particular features of a stimulus' (Allport, 1955 cited in Cassells and Green, 1991). Cassells and Green suggest nine factors which may influence this and elaborate on each one with reference to research related specifically to perceptual skills. All are relevant to the classroom and suggest possible ways for the teacher to use display as a tool for learning. Links with Gibson's (1969) perceptual strategies are also apparent.

The *context* in which children operate requires children to identify what they are seeing and relate it to experience and existing knowledge. Anything ambiguous or unclear, therefore, will hinder children's ability to make sense of what they see. Morgan and Welton (1986) claim that perception is selective and that attention is directed towards those aspects which have personal appeal or confirm prejudices.

Although it is beyond the scope of this chapter to consider in depth how children learn from *past experience*, (clearly linked to all four of Gibson's strategies) it is apparent that as children become perceptually selective they are more able to assimilate new information into their existing schema. They use their present understanding as a basis for extending that understanding as new opportunities are provided. However, if children are to learn from display it is not enough that they are merely positive about having their work included; they must also be sufficiently *motivated* to examine the display carefully and purposefully. When displays are planned as a resource rather than as an artefact, they become an integral part of the learning process.

Expectations and teacher instructions are also linked to Gibson's four strategies. If there is an alphabet frieze or a colour identification chart, for example, and the children know the teacher expects them to consult the charts before asking for help, they are more likely to use them successfully. Equally, of course, there may be a negative side to teacher expectations – children who are led to believe that their work is not neat enough or worthy enough to be included in a display will be unlikely to be interested in anything on the wall.

The use of instructions when children are producing work for a display has a direct influence on the outcome. This links with the teacher's expectations but also has relevance when the teacher informs the children in advance that their work may be displayed and gives additional instructions to facilitate this. If it is a negotiated decision between the teacher and the children, and the children feel they have ownership, they are likely to be better motivated than if the teacher tells them what to do and how to do it. (In particular, children are likely to be influenced, not necessarily in a positive way, if the teacher instructs them to work hard 'for me'). Instructions concerning how a display should be used may be very effective in developing children's perceptual skills. These might be verbal – encouraging children to seek out specific aspects of the display – or written in the form of labels. Displays produced solely by the teacher as a stimulus for future work by the children can also use labels to prompt exploration and discussion (Figure 4.2).

Figure 4.2 Displays created by the teacher as a stimulus for future work by the children. Labels prompt initial exploration and discussion of the topic.

Reward and punishment are clearly linked to teacher expectations, instructions and motivation. It seems unlikely that using sanctions would help children to develop their perceptual skills, but there are opportunities for rewarding effort, achievement and perseverance.

Gibson's third and fourth strategies are related to Cassell and Green's individual differences which refer, particularly in this context, to how far children are likely to be distracted by irrelevant aspects of the display. Some may need direct guidance to attend to the main focus. It could also refer to children's individual responses to specific displays and how the teacher uses this to take the child's understanding further.

Cultural factors are wide-ranging, particularly for children in a multi-cultural class. Equally, however, children would not necessarily make the connection between a picture of a cow next to a picture of a milk bottle if they had little or no experience of the countryside.

Arousing *emotions* can be achieved effectively through display, whether it is through explicit pictures designed to draw attention to particular situations (e.g. sad, puzzled, excited) or at a more subtle level – giving children a sense of pride in their work, perhaps (Figure 4.3, p.32).

Visual stimulation is of course the main purpose of advertising, for instance in packaging where the eye is drawn immediately to 'information about the nature of the contents' (Morgan and Welton 1986). Displays of children's work in classrooms are, in effect, the results of children's endeavours 'packaged' on the walls. The vital word in this analogy appears to be 'information' in its widest sense – not just 'content' but the coming together of children's past experience and understanding to create new meaning.

Although visual stimulation may be the most common and have the most impact through displays, stimulation of the other senses is also relevant. Three-dimensional displays which encourage children to use their sense of touch, taste, smell and hearing give opportunities for an increased awareness of the environment around them. Handling tactile, natural objects such as stones, shells, seaweed, feathers, grasses, wood, twisted roots or bark (Jackson 1993) can be balanced with man made objects of iron, steel, glass, plastic, or items which require problem solving skills: old clocks to dismantle and reassemble, tools which may be used for different purposes, circuit boards with bulbs and batteries, for instance. The important element here is touch and the information conveyed through touch; it is not merely a collection of attractive artefacts.

Similarly, taste and smell are powerful agents for learning. The fragrance of floral perfume sprayed on a summer display, for example, will evoke memories if smelled again, long after the visual display has been removed. Baking accompanied by relevant display work as a visual reminder can be effective for sustained memories of smell and taste, as well as awareness of heat and changes in materials.

Display which requires or encourages children to listen will have effects for further development of listening skills. Using a tape recorder, on which the teacher asks leading questions about the display will not only stimulate careful listening but will also focus children's attention onto pertinent aspects of the display. Incorporating buzzers, horns or bells into both two- and three-dimensional displays will encourage children to interact with them.

The plethora of potentially stimulating resources in the classroom is incorporated within Doyle's (1979) notion of the classroom as an information system. This includes both teacher's and children's verbal and non-verbal behaviour and the provision of books, displays, films and charts (Doyle, 1979; Bennett, 1984). Doyle contends that any of these resources 'may assume instructional significance, depending upon particular sets of circumstances' (Doyle, 1979:191). Doyle refers to the classroom as a 'mass-processing system' and acknowledges the problems inherent in this perspective. The way in which the classroom environment, including display, may impinge on and affect children's learning can be influenced by many different factors.

Visual factors such as quality of light, for example, acoustic factors including the impact of excessive noise and thermal factors which affect the comfort of the working environment (Bull and Solity, 1987) will all have an influence on the level of response which may be achieved through display.

Although some constraints may be difficult to reconcile, such as old buildings with display boards way above children's heads, teachers need perspectives from which to judge the effectiveness of display. Taylor (1986) suggests four fundamental standpoints for approaching art objects which could also be applied to display in classrooms. He contends that teachers can 'engage their pupils in fruitful conjecture in front of the art object' and proposes four areas for consideration – *content, form, process, mood*.

When considering the content, Taylor is concerned not solely with the physical outcome but with the intentions of the designer. In terms of displayed work produced by children it is worth pausing to consider whether the finished product is influenced by a 'hidden agenda' – pleasing the teacher, for example. Identification of specific areas of need, such as limited manipulative skills or specific areas of talent which might be developed, such as sensitive use of colour, may call for a modified approach when planning future work for children.

Taylor is also concerned with the degree to which paintings are treated representationally. This has different implications when applied to children's work and is an important aspect of their perceptual development. Making sense of their surroundings involves the related processes of recognition and categorization (Roth and Bruce, 1995). Small children may not differentiate between a table and a stool, for instance, because they have similar characteristics (a flat top and four legs), but as they grow older they can recognise the differences and categorize them.

Rumelhart and Norman (1985) highlight the need to 'distinguish between a *representing* world and a *represented* world. The representing world must somehow mirror some aspects of the represented world' (Roth and Bruce, 1995:195). Here, the represented world is the actual physical world surrounding the child and the cycle of three representing worlds discussed by Roth and Bruce is the process by which perception develops. These three representing worlds involve a cyclical process whereby some representations are stored in long-term memory, others are temporary intermediate stages in the processing of sensory input, and some are the final outcome of perceptual processing, as the ability to classify objects into conceptual categories increases. A typical example of this is the ability of a child to recognise and categorize a table as a table even if it has only three legs.

In the classroom, commercially produced alphabet friezes often include cartoon-type pictures of animals or objects, which most children are able to recognize and categorize. A typical picture of a house drawn by children is the front elevation – a flat square or rectangle with doors and windows. Other representations are equally 'flat'.

The ability to perceive objects as three dimensional can be developed through incorporating actual objects into wall displays and by opportunities for careful observational drawing (Figure 4.4, p.32). Examples of this include the use of real shells and pebbles for a seaside display or a real hat on a child-sized figure. Using actual objects also introduces enquiries about texture and size.

The appearance of a display and how it is produced (in Taylor's terms *form* and *process*) are fundamental elements which influence the impact on children. The layout or format of a display involves decisions about arrangement, size, shape, materials, contributions from individual children, joint efforts by groups of children and teacher-produced items. The overall effect may be harmonious or the display may consist of contrasts (Taylor, 1986). If the colour of the background is intrusive, the focus may be lost. Mortimer (1994) advocates the use of neutral backgrounds. The unity of the whole is important.

The choice of materials is particularly influential. Attention should be given to the qualities of the materials themselves, in addition to the impact they will have. Coloured tissue paper, for instance, has a wonderful floaty quality and is very effective for creating billowy clouds or the swell of the sea. It is sad to see these possibilities lost when it is screwed up tightly to make balls and glued onto an outline. This is totally at odds with the characteristics of tissue paper, and is of doubtful use as a learning experience.

The judicious use of labels to reinforce previous learning (new vocabulary, specific factual information) can provide 'trigger points' to attract children's attention. Written questions and instructions (and diagrams) related to the moving parts of the display encourage children to interact with it and provide opportunities for discussion to emphasise specific points for learning (Figure 4.5).

Shannon and Weaver's (1949) model of communication, which is 'widely accepted as one of the main seeds out of which Communication Studies has grown' (Fiske, 1990), identified three inter-connecting levels of problems for meaningful communication: *technical*, *semantic* and *effectiveness*. Relating these to the learning which might come about through display, technical problems could be interpreted as how accurately the information source (the teacher) transmits (displays) the means for learning (the communication). Semantic problems involve the need to transmit the message so that the desired meaning is achieved – in other words, the teacher must consciously select the most appropriate method and format for the display to promote the desired learning. Shannon and Weaver's third level, effectiveness problems, is concerned with how effectively the messages received 'affect conduct in the desired way' (Fiske, 1990). Fiske criticizes this aspect of the model, contending that communication is thus portrayed as manipulative, but in the classroom intentional outcomes for learning are necessary and this criticism may not be applicable in this context.

Figure 4.5 Written questions and instructions encourage children to interact with the display and explore their existing knowledge and understanding

A further aspect of the model is *noise*. Shannon and Weaver's theory was developed while working on telephone communication so *noise* was intended to be literally noise, but the meaning has been extended to refer to distractions experienced by the recipient of the communication which will interfere with the desired message. Thus, children who are unable to ignore irrelevant information (Gibson, 1969), may not receive the teacher's intended messages – that is, intended learning opportunities.

Although Shannon and Weaver identify the levels as *problems*, they need not be so when applied to communication through display. They can be used to provide teachers with a simple checklist for planning and evaluating effective displays. Similarly, if children are the decision makers in planning and executing display, the levels might be used in discussion with the teacher as a starting point for identifying purpose, audience and format.

Planning displays can present teachers with dilemmas as the final outcome needs to fulfil different and sometimes conflicting criteria. Having determined the subject matter, decisions must be made about appropriate materials, tools and techniques (Taylor 1986), taking availability into account. Children's work to be displayed may be spontaneous or it may be pre-planned (by the teacher or by the children with guidance from the teacher), drafted and refined, either by the teacher or the children. This leads to the tricky question of how far the finished display should be pre-conceived in the teacher's mind before it is started.

The need to reconcile pre-planned opportunities for learning with the need for children to have communal ownership of their classrooms, including display (Coulby and Coulby 1990), can lead to conflict of purpose. This may be another reason for developing and extending displays so that their first form is not the final one. Teachers are then able to change or emphasise the main focus and sustain interest and involvement not only through their own intervention, but also by acting on suggestions from the children.

In addition to the development of cognitive skills, affective responses are worth noting. Developing perceptual skills through stimulation of the emotions (Cassells and Green, 1991) is taken further in Taylor's (1986) final point, *mood*. Taylor suggests that emotional reaction can be extended by examining the particular qualities of the picture which has aroused the emotions and exploring reasons for the reaction. He also suggests that the feelings of the artist should be surmised – or in this context, they could form the basis for group or class discussion (Figure 4.6, p.32). This would serve the purpose of giving the teacher opportunities to reinforce specific areas of learning connected with the display, but also give rise to development in other curriculum areas.

The National Curriculum (1995) Programmes of Study for Art at Key Stage 1 include the need to develop visual perception, where

> pupils should be taught the creative, imaginative and practical skills needed to:
>
> a) express ideas and feelings;
>
> b) record observations;
>
> c) design and make images and artefacts.

At Key Stages 1 and 2, development of visual literacy should be facilitated through teaching children 'about the different ways in which ideas, feelings and meanings are communicated in visual form'. Relevant, well-presented display incorporates not only the 'doing' but also the opportunity for all these requirements to be fulfilled.

CHILDREN'S VIEWPOINTS

During my classroom visits as tutor to student teachers I had the opportunity to talk informally with individual children and small groups of children. My purpose was to investigate the children's perceptions of the displays in their classrooms and of the opportunities for learning from the displays. In particular, the four perceptual strategies proposed by Gibson (1969) and the three strategies for stimulation suggested by Pollard and Tann (1987), outlined earlier in the chapter, were used as a framework for the analysis and interpretation of the children's responses.

From the range of individual cases studied, three have been selected to illustrate the perceptual strategies suggested by Gibson (1969) and Pollard and Tann (1987) and to give specific contexts to the more general points which emerge. The three case studies which follow represent different classroom situations with different kinds of display. Each has been selected to highlight issues relevant to the development of visual perception and which give some insight into how children perceive display in the classroom.

Sally (Reception)

'That's mine, the one with the green on it'.

Sally pointed to a paper plate, in a row of similar plates, which had eyes, nose, mouth and hair glued onto them to depict faces. There were no name labels under the plates and there was nothing green on Sally's plate.

'It's me ' she said, 'I've got brown hair'.

The woollen hair was brown. Sally had enjoyed making the face because 'I like sticking things on'. She didn't know why they had made them but she thought they looked nice on the wall. She pointed out her friend's face,

Figure 4.7 An example of ways in which learning can be extended through work designed to build on an existing display

announcing that it was good; she was unable to say why it was good except that it was made by her friend.

Sally could identify the features on the faces and questioning revealed that she also knew the names of other body parts – knees, elbows etc. as well as main parts such as arms and legs. Unsurprisingly, Sally could not read the label – *Ourselves* – above the row of faces. When asked, she did not know how many eyes people have, but she could count them on the plates when invited to do so. She went along the row of plates counting 'One, two', touching the eyes on each plate as she did so. When she reached the end of the row she was asked again how many eyes we have. 'Two' she replied, confidently, and touched her own eyes. 'One, two'.

The display was effectively positioned low down on the wall, which enabled Sally to touch it – it is unlikely that she could have counted the eyes simply by pointing in the air if the row of plates had been higher.

As Sally knew the names of body parts like elbows and knees she was probably familiar with eyes, nose, mouth and hair before she made her face. None of the plates included eyebrows, eyelashes or ears! Although she is only four years old, it seems likely that Sally could have included these if the idea had been suggested to her, using a mirror for careful observation, helping to develop her perceptual skills.

Sally could count to two (the maximum number needed for this activity) but she did not *know* that people have two eyes. She was also unsure of colours – she thought the blue eyes on her plate were called green. The addition of cards depicting pairs of eyes, labelled '2 blue eyes', '2 brown eyes' or '1 nose' and '1 mouth' would extend this display and take the children's learning on.

Sally did not know why she had decorated the plate – was she aware of the connection between the current topic of *Ourselves* and the actual activity? She knew 'It's me' but was unaware of what was coming next.

Stuart (Year 5)

Stuart's classroom, although bright and welcoming, was small and crowded. The children's tables were close together and some children, including Stuart, were sitting at tables pushed against the wall. When asked for his views on the displays round the room, Stuart replied 'I only see this one', indicating the small section of wall directly in front of him. Although there were examples of his work in other parts of the room, he said that he did not 'bother much' to look at them or at any other displayed work. He was uninterested and thought that there was 'not much point' in having work displayed in the classroom. Stuart said he was 'too busy doing my work' to pay any attention to his surroundings.

Other children in the class, sitting in more fortunate positions, were more positive than Stuart, but not unduly so. There was an element of competition evident in some comments referring to whose work was superior and whose was less good.

It is impossible to gauge the extent to which Stuart's physical position in the classroom influenced his attitude towards display, although it is certainly true that his vision was severely restricted by the size of the classroom, the layout of the furniture and the fact that he was facing the wall. The opportunities for developing his visual perceptual skills were, therefore, minimal unless interaction with displays had been consciously built into the teacher's planning.

None of the other children, chosen at random, appeared particularly interested or impressed by the displays. The displays themselves looked a little 'tired', indicating perhaps that they had been in place for some time. The children appeared rather surprised to be asked about the displays as if this was not a common occurrence. This suggests that the teacher regarded display as low priority and that this was reflected in the children's attitudes.

Helen (Year 3)

The notion of intended audience for display was explored with Helen. When asked why she thought the display had been put up, she replied that it was for visitors to see what the children had been doing. She elaborated on this by saying it would be especially good if the visitors were 'important' because a reporter from the local newspaper would probably attend and 'write good things about the school in the paper'.

Helen did not believe the displays had been created for the children; she was clearly surprised at this suggestion. 'Mrs. A. does them', she said, referring to the teacher. She obviously thought this explained everything. Helen preferred the display which contained work completed mostly by herself and the children in her group. It was a source of slight annoyance to her that the composition of the group had been changed since the display was finished so it was not now an accurate record of her current group's activities.

The children were not given any choice of what should be displayed or whose work would be included. Asked if she would like to be involved in these decisions sometimes, Helen was enthusiastic. She said she would choose 'good work' but was unable to expand on how she would decide what was good work. She added that she would include more of her own work if given the opportunity. Other children in Helen's group were equally keen to be involved but for different reasons. David wanted to include work from every child in the class, whereas Amy thought only 'neat stuff without marks on' (meaning smudges) should be displayed.

They were all agreed that they looked at the displays 'sometimes' but were unsure whether the displays helped them to remember work covered previously. It did appear, however, that as their attention was drawn to specific aspects of a display and they were asked for comments or explanations, that there were 'trigger points' on the display which jogged their memories. It was noticeable that the children could remember what they had done and what they had been trying to find out, but that the related vocabulary had been forgotten. One display discussed by the group contained cut-outs of hands, accompanied by labels incorporating words such as 'digits' and 'spans'. The children read the words aloud and debated amongst themselves until they were satisfied that they had remembered the meanings correctly.

The displays covered a variety of topics and were presented attractively, including neatly written or computer-produced labels featuring single key words, questions, instructions and factual information. Helen had her own definite idea of the purpose of the displays and valued them for that reason.

All the children in Helen's group had their own ideas about what should be included in displays and all claimed to look at them 'sometimes'. When asked about the content, they were able to explain what the work had involved, although some of the vocabulary needed revision. They were all able to discriminate between different aspects of the display and relate them to their own experience. Perceptual skills were developed to the point where they could focus on specific points in the displays and use them to recall previous learning.

SUMMARY

All the children, including 4-year-old Sally, were able to use Gibson's (1969) *capture to activity* perceptual strategy, whereby intention and interest will influence what is perceived. Indeed, Sally was the only child who drew attention to the display without being asked about it, making specific reference to her own work. This motivation was not immediately apparent from any of the other children, although Helen and her group were aware of the activities which preceded the display and were keen to talk about it when asked to do so. Stuart showed no motivation to approach displays or to discuss them.

Gibson's second strategy *less systematic to more systematic search* was demonstrated by Sally, as she was able to find her own work, and that of her friend, from the long row of faces on the wall. Stuart knew where his work was displayed in the room even though he was not very interested. Helen and her group demonstrated both this strategy and Gibson's third strategy, *broad to selective pick-up of information*. There were several eye-catching displays in the classroom and Helen chose to discuss the one created mainly by her group. She did not need to move closer to the display in order to point out specific aspects of it, how the parts had been put together and who had created them.

Gibson's fourth strategy, *ignoring irrelevant information*, is more difficult to categorise. Sally's display was very simple, containing no extraneous material. Stuart could see only one or two pictures directly in front of him; he was unable to see a display as an entity. The displays in Helen's classroom were busy and full of information. There was no apparent focal point so there was no way of telling whether there were particular aspects on which the teacher wished the children to concentrate. The labels were thought provoking but were arranged in such a way that it was not possible to identify the key ones – none of them were presented in larger, brighter or darker lettering, on eye-catching background cards or in 3-dimensional form. It might be concluded from this that there was not any 'irrelevant information' but also that there were not any key points highlighted as specific pegs for learning.

Pollard and Tann's (1987) *capitilizing on children's interests and experience* was clearly evident in Sally's display. She was delighted to point out her own face ('It's me') and that of her friend. Stuart's physical position meant that he was excluded in visual terms, but other children in the class also showed some lack of interest, indicating perhaps that they had not had the opportunity to develop perceptual skills in this way. Helen and the children in her group were interested in the display partly because it consisted mainly of their own work, and were thoughtful in their reconstruction of the learning involved. They investigated the forgotten vocabulary without prompting and worked actively together to recall previous understanding.

Pollard and Tann's *challenging children to investigate* and *channelling their curiosity* were not overtly evident in any of the displays. Opportunities for interaction through hands-on experience (such as flaps, pulleys and levers) were not in evidence in any of the three classrooms. This was also true in most of the other classrooms not described in the case studies. The use of labelling for Helen's group was clearly effective in provoking discussion, but not all the children in the class had such well developed reading skills.

CONCLUSION

The main message which emerges from a consideration of the development of children's perceptual skills and their perception of displays in the classroom is one of opportunities. Displays are a rich source of potential learning, but only if that potential is exploited. Integrating the *use* of display into planning, as well as merely the *intention to produce* display, is necessary if the possibilities for learning are to be maximised. Three main headings could be used as a starting point: *purpose, audience, format.*

Consideration of the purpose of a display includes recognition of the potential for learning. It includes clear links between the learning intentions for the tasks which the children undertake in order to produce the display and development of those learning intentions from the display itself. Also

Figure 4.8 Identification of the main focus for learning leads to a simple, clear message for the children

instrumental in the decision-making process of planning display is the amount and nature of teacher input, and how this will be balanced with the degree of ownership the children will have. Children need to know that they are the main audience and need encouragement to behave like an audience in any other context – to pay attention and to have considered opinions about the quality of what they see and what they gain from it.

The tension between pre-conceived notions of a finished display and the need for on-going, developing display influences the choice of format. Identification of the main focus for learning and decisions about how this focus can have the necessary impact may be made by the teacher alone or in consultation with the children (Figure 4.8). The quality of presentation reflects the efforts and achievement of the children in producing the work included in the display.

Just as children's perceptual skills develop through stimulation of the senses, so the teacher uses her own senses to raise awareness of the children's responses to display. If the children's reactions are less than enthusiastic, if they are not interacting with the display, if the learning is not apparent, then perhaps the display is not so much an opportunity for learning as an opportunity missed.

AFTERWORD

I am writing this some three months after we submitted the manuscript of *Display in the Classroom* to our publisher.

In the Introduction I placed A.H. Garlick's thoughts on classroom environments (published in 1896) with our students' contemporary concerns with the technical details of creating displays and with making connections to theories about how children learn and thrive.

At the beginning of the autumn term I asked my students, who were starting their teaching practice, to record and evaluate their displays on a short version of the forms in the tables in Chapter 1. Rebecca Newton, devising a display to accompany Year 5's unit on Vikings, did just that, and also listened to the children as they talked. The child who prepared the heading 'What can you find out about Vikings? badgered her mum to take her to join the public library so that she could 'find out'. The librarian then ordered more books from another branch, much to this scholar's delight. The classroom teacher volunteered that she had not been taught about display at all when she did her teacher training and was pleased to be involved in this new strategy.

This brief episode illuminated for us, once more, the ways that thoughtful and reflective approaches to display can enliven and extend learning in practical, formative and rewarding ways.

We also began the book by expressing our anxiety that current emphasis on economy, core subjects, league tables and detailed accounting for curriculum hours might mean that display is given a low priority. We were therefore pleased to read an article by Jonathan Foster in the *Independent* (6 February 1996) about Bethune Primary School in Hull, which recently received an 'excellent' OFSTED report. In this article the buildings are described as 'cheapskate 1960s single-storey blocks ... hardly an inspiration ... but inside the walls are startlingly lucid'. The headteacher, Maureen Mather, has increased the budget for display to ensure the most vivid presentation possible for work, 'something the Inspectors found very impressive during their visit last January'. This is an encouraging conclusion to our book.

Hilary Cooper
February 1996

REFERENCES

Ainscow, M. and Tweddle, D.A. (1988) *Encouraging Classroom Success* London: David Fulton.

Allport, G.W. (1955) *Becoming* New Haven: Yale University Press.

Armitage, R. and Armitage, D. (1977) *The Lighthouse Keeper's Lunch* London: Andre Deutsch.

Arnheim, R. (1974) *Art and Visual Perception* Berkley: University Conference Press.

Ausubel, D.P. (1963) *The Psychology of Meaningful Verbal Learning* New York: Greene and Stratton.

Ausubel, D.P. (1968) *Educational Psychology: A Cognitive View* London: Holt, Rinehart and Winston.

Beales, A.C.F. (1995) The historical development of "activity methods" in education. *Pedagogica* Conference Paper, Louvain, and *National Froebel Foundation Bulletin* 106, June 1957

Bennett, S.N., Desforges, C., Cockburn, A. and Wilkinson, B. (1984) *The Quality of Pupil Learning Experiences* Hove: Erlbaum.

Bevis, A.W. (1895) *A Course of Practical Lessons on Hand and Eye Training* London: Newmann.

Bloom, B.S. (1976) *Human Characteristics and School Learning* New York: McGraw-Hill.

Bower, T. (1977) *The Perceptual World of the Child* London: Open Books.

Bruner, J.S. (1963) *The Process of Education* New York: Vintage Books.

Bruner, J.S. (1966) *Towards a Theory of Instruction* Cambridge, MA: Belknap Press.

Bruner, J.S. (1983) *Child's Talk: Learning to Use Language* Oxford: Oxford University Press.

Bruner, J.S. (1986) *Actual Minds: Possible Worlds* Cambridge MA: Harvard University Press.

Bull, S.L. and Solity, J.E. (1987) *Classroom Management: Principles to Practice* London: Routledge

Cassells, A. and Green, P. (1991) *Perception* London: British Psychological Society.

Corbin, T. (1970) *Displays in Schools* Kidlington: Pergamon.

Coulby, J. and Coulby, D. in Docking, J. (1990) *Managing Behaviour in the Primary School* London: David Fulton

Department of Education and Science (1967) *Children and their Primary Schools: A Report of the Central Advisory Council for Education* (The Plowden Report) London: HMSO.

Department of Education and Science (1989) *Aspects of Primary Education: The Education of Children Under Five* London: HMSO.

Department for Education (1995) *Art in the National Curriculum* London: DFE Publication Centre.

Desforges, C. and Cockburn, A. (1987) *Understanding the Mathematics Teacher: A Study of Practice in First Schools* Lewes: Falmer Press.

Doise, W., Mugny, G. and Perret Clermont, A.N. (1975) Social interaction and the development of cognitive operations. *European Journal of Social Psychology*, 5:367–83.

Donaldson, M. (1978) *Children's Minds* London: Fontana.

Doyle, W. (1977) Learning the environment: an ecological analysis. *Journal of Teacher Education*, 28, (6): 51–55

Doyle, W. (1979) Classroom tasks and students' abilities. In P.L. Peterson and H.J. Walberg (eds) *Research on Teaching: Concepts, Findings and Implications*. Berkeley: McCutchan (183–209).

Doyle, W. (1983) Academic work. *Review of Educational Research*, 52: 159–199.

Doyle, W. (1986) Classroom organization and management. In M.C. Whitrock (ed.) *Handbook of Research on Teaching*. New York: Macmillan.

Fantz, R.L. (1961) The origin of form perception *Scientific American*, 204: 66–72.

Fantz, R.L. (1963) Pattern vision in newborn infants *Science*, 140: 266–7.

Fenstermacher, G. (1980) "On learning to teach effectively", from Research on Teacher Effectiveness. In C. Denham, and A. Lieberman (eds), *Time to Learn:* Department of Education/NFE, Washington, pp 127–137.

Fiske, J. (1990) *Introduction to Communication Studies* (2nd edn) London: Routledge.

Gagne, R.M. (1977) *Conditions of Learning*. New York: Holt, Rinehart and Winston.

Galton, M. (1989) *Teaching in the Primary School* London: David Fulton.

Galton, M. (1995) *Crisis in the Primary Classroom* London: David Fulton.

Garlick, A.H. (1896) *New Manual of Method* London: Longman, Green.

Gauvain, M. and Rogoff, B. (1989) Collaborative problem solving and children's planning skills. *Developmental Psychology* 25 (1): 139–151.

Gibson, E.J. (1969) *Principles of Perceptual Learning and Development* Englewood Cliffs: Prentice-Hall.

Goodrow, J.J. (1977) *Children Drawing* Cambridge MA: Harvard University Press.

Goodrow, J.J. (1978) Visual thinking: cognitive aspects of change in drawing. *Child Development* 49: 637–41.

Gopne, R.M. (1977) *The Conditions of Learning* London: Rinehart and Winston.

Goren, C.C. (1975) Visual following and pattern discrimination of face-like stimuli of newborn infants. *Pediatrics* (56): 544–9.

Greenstreet, D. (1985) *Ways to Display: A Practical Guide for Teachers* London: Ward Lock Educational.

Guilford, J.P. (1959) Traits of creativity. In H.H. Anderson (ed) *Creativity and its Cultivation*. New York: Harper.

Hall, N. and Abbott, L. (1991) *Play in the Primary Curriculum* London: Hodder and Stoughton.

Hart, S. (1992) Collaborative classrooms. In T. Booth, W. Swann, M. Masterton and P. Potts. (eds), *Curriculum for Diversity in Education*. London: Routledge.

Housego, E. and Burns, C. (1994) Are you sitting too comfortably? a critical look at circle time in primary classrooms. *English in Education*, 28(2): 23–29.

Ingram, J. and Worrall, N. (1993) *Teacher–Child Partnership: The Negotiating Classroom* London: David Fulton.

Isaacs, S. (1930) *Intellectual Growth in Young Children* London: Routledge and Kegan Paul.

Jackson, M. (1993) *Creative Display and Environment*. London: Hodder and Stoughton.

Kellogg, R. (1967) *Analysing Children's Art* Palo Alto: Mayfield.

Klausmeier, M.J. and Allen, P.S. (1978) *Cognitive Development of Children and Youth: A Longitudinal Study* London: Academic Press.

Klausmeier, H.J. (1979) *Cognitive Learning and Development* Cambridge MA: Ballinger.

Makoff, J. and Duncan, L. (1990) *A World of Display Topics Across the Curriculum for Infants and Lower Juniors* Twickenham: Belair.

Marshall, S. (1963) *An Experiment in Education* Cambridge: Cambridge University Press.

Matthews, J. (1983) Children's drawing: are young children really scribbling? Paper presented at the British Psychological Society International Conference on Psychology and the Arts, Cardiff.

Mead, G.H. (1934) *Mind, Self and Society* Chicago: University of Chicago Press.

Morgan, J. and Welton, P. (1986) *See What I Mean* London: Hodder and Stoughton.

Mortimer, A.R. (1994) Display and the learning environment. Unpublished paper, Department of Teaching and Education Studies, Lancaster University.

Moyles, J.R. (1989) *Just Playing? The Role and Status of Play in Early Childhood* Milton Keynes: Open University Press.

Perret Clermont, A.N. (1980) *Social Interaction and Cognitive Development in Children* London: Academic Press.

Piaget, J. (1951) *Play, Dreams and Imitation in Childhood* London: Heinemann.

Piaget, J. (1954) *The Construction of Reality in the Child* New York: Ballantine.

Piaget, J. and Inhelder, B. (1956) *The Child's Conception of Space* London: Routledge and Kegan Paul.

Pollard, A. (1985) *The Social World of the Primary School* London: Holt, Rinehart and Winston.

Pollard, A. and Tann, S. (1987) *Reflective Teaching in the Primary School* London: Cassell.

Radziszewska, B. and Rogoff, B. (1991) Children's guided participation in planning imaginary errands with skilled adults or peer partners. *Development Psychology* 27 (3): 381–9.

Raths, J.D. (1971) Teaching without specific objectives. *Educational Leadership*, April, 714–20.

Roth, I. and Bruce, V. (1995) *Perception and Representation* (2nd edn) London: Routledge.

Rowland, S. (1987) Child in control: towards an interpretive model of teaching and learning. In A. Pollard (ed.), *Children and Their Primary Schools* London: Falmer.

Rumelhart, D.E. and Normal, D.A. (1985) Representation of knowledge. In A.M. Aitkenhead and J.M. Slack, (eds) *Issues in Cognitive Modelling*. Hove: Erlbaum.

Schön, D. (1987) *Educating the Reflective Practitioner*. San Francisco: Jossey-Bass.

Schools Council Art Committee (1978) *Art 7–11*. London: Schools Council.

Shannon, C. and Weaver, W. (1949) in Fiske, J. (1990) *Introduction to Communication Studies* (2nd edn) London: Routledge

Shannon, C. and Weaver, W. (1949) *The Mathematical Theory of Communication*. Chicago: University of Illinois Press.

Silcock, P.J. (1993) Towards a new progressivism in primary school education. *Educational Studies*, 19(1): 107–21.

Silcock, P. (1994) Modern progressivism: a way forward for the 1993 ASPE Conference. *Education* 22(2): 3–13.

Simco, N.P. (1995) Using activity analysis to investigate primary classroom environments. *British Educational Research Journal*, 21(1): 49–60.

Sylva, K. and Lunt, I. (1982) *Child Development: A First Course* Oxford: Blackwell.

Taylor, R. (1986) *Educating for Art: Critical Response and Development* London: Longman.

Torrance, E.P. (1965) *Rewarding Creative Behavior*. New York: Prentice Hall.

Tudge, J.R.H. (1992) Processes and consequences of peer collaboration: a Vygotsky analysis. *Child Development* 63: 1364–79.

Vygotsky, L.S. (1962) *Thought and Language* Chichester: Wiley.

Vygotsky, L.S. (1978) *Mind in Society* Cambridge, MA: Harvard University Press.

Warham, S.M. (1993) *Primary Teaching and the Negotiation of Power* London: Chapman.

Wertheimer, M. (1961) Psychomotor co-ordination of auditory-visual space at birth. *Science*, 134: 1692.

Willats, J. (1981) What do the marks on the paper stand for? the child's acquisition of systems of transformation and denotation. *Review of Research in Visual Arts Education*, 13: 18–33.

Woods, P. (ed.) (1980) *Pupil Strategies* London: Croom Helm.

Woods, P. (1990) *The Happiest Days?* London: Falmer.

Wragg, E.C. (1993) *Primary Teaching Skills* London: Routledge.

Index